Release,
Rest,
Remain

Release, Rest, Remain

A 30-Day Devotional
to Embrace Abiding
Over Striving

Yvette Henry

WATERBROOK

WaterBrook

An imprint of the Penguin Random House Christian Publishing Group,
a division of Penguin Random House LLC
1745 Broadway, New York, NY 10019

waterbrookmultnomah.com
penguinrandomhouse.com

Library of Congress Cataloging-in-Publication Data
Names: Henry, Yvette, author.
Title: Release, rest, remain / Yvette Henry.
Description: New York, NY: WaterBrook, [2026] | Includes bibliographical references.
Identifiers: LCCN 2025025140 (print) | LCCN 2025025141 (ebook) |
ISBN 9780593602973 (hardcover) | ISBN 9780593602980 (ebook)
Subjects: LCSH: Peace of mind—Religious aspects—Christianity. |
Joy—Religious aspects—Christianity. | Christian women—Religious life.
Classification: LCC BV4908.5 .H457 2026 (print) | LCC BV4908.5 (ebook)
LC record available at https://lccn.loc.gov/2025025140
LC ebook record available at https://lccn.loc.gov/2025025141

Printed in the United States of America

1st Printing

FIRST EDITION

The authorized representative in the EU for product safety and compliance
is Penguin Random House Ireland, Morrison Chambers, 32 Nassau Street,
Dublin D02 YH68, Ireland. https://eu-contact.penguin.ie

BOOKMAKING TEAM: Production editor: Helen Macdonald • Managing editor: Julia Wallace •
Production manager: Maggie Hart • Copy editor: Rose Decaen •
Proofreaders: Lisa Grimenstein, Andrew Buss

Leaf illustration: Oleksandra/Adobe Stock
Part-opening illustrations: RJ Vergara

For details on special quantity discounts for bulk purchases,
contact specialmarketscms@penguinrandomhouse.com.

To Glen, Theo, Uriah, Anaya, and Uzi:
You are my greatest earthly reminder of God's faithfulness.
Thank you for the laughter that lightens my heart,
the grace that lifts my burdens, and the love
that teaches me daily what it means to remain.

Contents

First, Breathe . . .

don't know what it took for you to carve out this moment. Maybe sitting with this book open on your lap meant leaving the full inbox that demands your attention, taking a much-needed break from your children, or ignoring the endless list of things you didn't quite check off today. Maybe you had to push past the pull of distraction, fight through the weight of worry, or resist the exhaustion that comes from feeling like you're always running behind. Whatever sacrifice or struggle brought you here, I want to acknowledge it, because I know what it's like to carry all the things.

Before we begin, let's pause and take a deep breath.

Inhale for four seconds . . .

Hold for four seconds . . .

Exhale for four seconds . . .

Hold for four seconds . . .

Let's do it again.

Inhale . . .

Hold . . .

Exhale . . .

Hold . . .

If you need to, repeat this as many times as it takes for your shoulders to relax, for the tension in your jaw to ease, for your heart rate to slow just a little. You made it here.

And my encouragement to you is this: Be fully here.

This devotional isn't something to rush through, another task to check off before moving on to the next thing. You are invited to slow down and be with Jesus, who doesn't demand more of you but instead asks you to lay things down.

Rest and remain in My presence and allow Me to do the rest.

A few years ago, I found myself trapped in a cycle of anxious striving. I was trying to check every box, meet every expectation, and hold everything together. The doing, proving, and striving left me exhausted, constantly pursuing rest but never quite arriving. I didn't realize how much I was carrying until I finally stepped away to spend time in stillness with my Abba.

In the quiet, I felt the Lord pressing something onto my heart. A simple invitation: *Rest and remain in My presence and allow Me to do the rest.*

At first, His call was just a whisper in my spirit, a gentle nudge. But when I felt anxiety fill my heart, I found myself coming back to it—rest and remain. With time, the invitation became clearer. Before I could truly rest, I had to release. I had to let go of the things that were never mine to carry in the first place. The need for control. The pressure to be enough. The fears that kept me from trusting God completely.

When I arrived at that place of surrender, rest became possible. A rest rooted not in the absence of struggle but in the presence of a God who holds everything together. A rest that isn't passive but deeply reliant on who He says He is.

I would release, find rest, then try to pick up things I had already laid down at the feet of Jesus. I learned to release, assume the posture of rest, and remain there. And as I remained, I began to see that remaining was an active choice to trust God, even when I felt pulled to take it all back. And then I'd do it all over again.

Release, rest, remain . . . repeat.

This became my rhythm. And over time, I found myself sharing it, not just as encouragement but as a lifeline. I've whispered these words to weary friends, to anxious hearts, and to myself in the middle of the night: *Release, rest, remain.*

And that's why we're here: to learn how to live this out. As we step into this thirty-day journey, we'll go back to where God first revealed this rhythm to me: John 15, which recounts Jesus's last moments with His disciples.

On that holy night, Jesus felt the weight of what was coming. He had washed the disciples' feet, broken bread with them, and spoken of His coming departure. Now, late in the evening and just after the Passover meal, they walked through the darkened streets toward the Garden of Gethsemane. Jesus spoke of vines and branches, of abiding love and lasting fruit. Words that weren't about doing but about *being*—about dwelling close to Him when everything else would tell them to run. "Abide in Me," He said. "Rest in My love. Remain in Me."

In this devotional, you'll walk the same path the disciples did, using the gift of time to study Jesus's words. You'll spend ten days in each section—Release, Rest, and Remain—but you'll find that these aren't rigid categories. They don't exist in isolation; they move together in harmony, much like the notes of a melody. You might release something today, but tomorrow you'll find yourself needing to lay it down again. You may arrive at rest, only to realize that true rest requires trust. A trust that keeps pulling you back to His presence when you're tempted to pick up burdens again. And when you remain, you will see just how often you are tempted to wander and how much intentionality it takes to stay rooted in Him.

Think of it like a song.

A melody isn't just one note played over and over—it's a sequence of sounds, movements, and harmonies that create something beautiful. In the same way, release, rest, and remain isn't a destination—it's a rhythm we follow.

So as we begin this journey together, I want to remind you: This is not about perfection. It's about presence.

You don't have to get it all right. You don't have to force anything to happen. You are simply invited to show up, open your heart, and let God lead you in this rhythm, one breath, one release, one moment of rest at a time. And as you do, remain with Him, letting His presence be the place you return to again and again.

Release

Day 1

The gym smelled like rubber and determination. The air was thick with the sound of weights hitting the floor, the steady rhythm of breath control, and the occasional encouragement from our trainer.

I was in the zone. Checking my form in the mirror, I watched as my body moved with precision—squat, swing, breathe, repeat. My leggings and tank top clung to my frame, damp with sweat, but I felt strong. My kettlebell was heavy, but it was mine. I had control.

Then I glanced over at my husband.

Seriously?!

Effortless. Relaxed. He swung his kettlebell like it was weightless, like he was tossing a set of keys in the air. My competitive side flared.

If he can throw that thing around like it's nothing, surely I can pick it up.

So, in a moment of completely unearned confidence, I walked over to his weight. I planted my feet, gripped the handle, and pulled.

Nothing.

Okay, maybe my form was off. I reset, making sure my feet were grounded. I bent my knees, engaged my core, and tried again. This time, I got the kettlebell off the ground, but that was as far as I got. My arms refused to lift it any higher. Swinging it through the air? Not happening.

Meanwhile, my husband—completely unbothered—finally noticed what I was doing. One eyebrow raised, his face said everything: *Why would you even try?*

It was then that I had a revelation: *His weight was never meant for me to carry.*

That moment in the gym was humbling. But isn't that just like life?

We carry so much—worries about the future, the weight of people's opinions, and the pressure to meet the never-ending demands of daily life. We carry the responsibility of provision, making sure everyone is taken care of, from our families to our co-workers to the friend who always seems to need one more thing from us. We carry the pressure to keep it all together, to be the reliable one, the strong one, the one who makes it look effortless.

And now, in this digital age, we carry even more. We are constantly aware of the heaviness of the world—the tragedies, the injustices, the suffering of people we will never meet but still grieve for. It's an unbearable load, yet we convince ourselves we have to hold it all. We push ourselves past our limits, refusing to release what is too heavy.

But here's the thing: We were never meant to carry the weight of the world.

Jesus knows our tendency to carry weights we were never meant to bear. He knew it about His disciples too.

For three years, the disciples' lives had revolved around Jesus.

They had left everything to follow Him—their jobs, their routines, their sense of stability. He was their teacher, their leader, their friend. But now, as they walked with Jesus after the Passover meal, He was telling them that He was leaving.

I imagine His words must have settled heavy on their hearts. They had watched miracles unfold, heard truth straight from His lips, and built their lives around His presence. And now He was preparing them for a reality in which He would no longer walk beside them.

They couldn't cling to the vine while holding on to everything else.

To step into what was next, they had to release their expectations of how things were supposed to go, their fear of an unknown future, and their desire to hold on to Jesus as they had always known Him. Would they be able to let go of control and trust that, even in His absence, He was still guiding them?

As they walked toward the Garden of Gethsemane, Jesus didn't hand them a step-by-step plan or a list of rules to follow. Instead, He gave them a picture of a vine and its branches.

> Remain in me, and I in you. Just as a branch is unable to produce fruit by itself unless it remains on the vine, neither can you unless you remain in me. (John 15:4)

He spoke words that would stay with them long after He was gone. Words about remaining, abiding, and bearing fruit. But beneath those words was an unspoken invitation to release. Because to remain in Him, they would have to let go of everything that kept them from staying connected. They couldn't cling to the vine while holding on to everything else.

Have you ever been there? I've been there more times than I can count. And what I've come to realize is that I can't force myself to release anything without first trusting the One I'm releasing it to.

We often resist release because it feels like losing control. But what if release isn't about loss? What if it's about making room? What if letting go isn't falling? What if it's finally being held?

This is the starting point of our rhythm. Before we can rest, before we can remain, we must release.

Over the next nine days, we'll explore the things we keep holding on to—fear, control, expectations, self-reliance—and what happens when we finally let them go. We'll wrestle with questions like:

- What fears keep us from releasing control?

- Why do we struggle to surrender our expectations?

- What happens when we resist the pruning process?

- How does abiding in Jesus help us release?

- How does releasing lead to true spiritual rest?

We'll spend time in John 15:1–8, lingering over Jesus's words and what they teach us about release. Each day will take us deeper into this passage, inviting us to let go of what is keeping us from fully abiding in Him.

Does digging deeper feel overwhelming? Are you already stressing over the questions we'll wrestle with? Exhale, friend. You don't need to figure everything out. Letting go doesn't begin with your achievements or efforts. It begins with God's presence. Today isn't about forcing your way forward; it's about leaning into the One who never lets go.

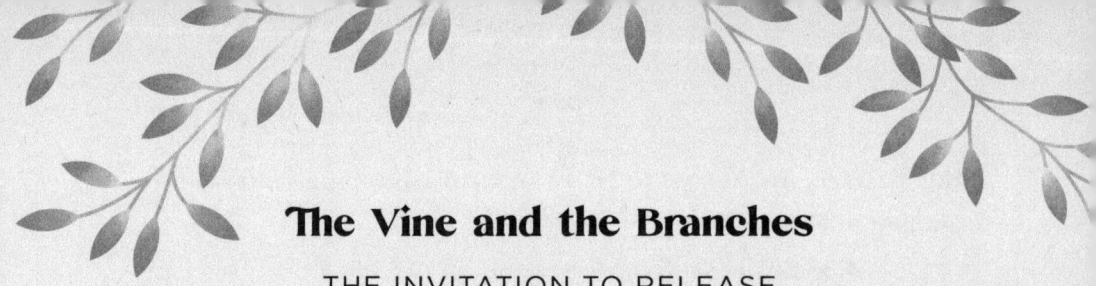

The Vine and the Branches

THE INVITATION TO RELEASE

Read these words from the beginning of John 15. Imagine yourself walking with Jesus. It's late, the air is still, and He turns to look at you as He speaks. His words aren't rushed. He knows exactly what you need to hear.

> *I am the true vine, and my Father is the gardener. Every branch in me that does not produce fruit he removes, and he prunes every branch that produces fruit so that it will produce more fruit. You are already clean because of the word I have spoken to you. Remain in me, and I in you. Just as a branch is unable to produce fruit by itself unless it remains on the vine, neither can you unless you remain in me. I am the vine; you are the branches. The one who remains in me and I in him produces much fruit, because you can do nothing without me. If anyone does not remain in me, he is thrown aside like a branch and he withers. They gather them, throw them into the fire, and they are burned. If you remain in me and my words remain in you, ask whatever you want and it will be done for you. My Father is glorified by this: that you produce much fruit and prove to be my disciples. (verses 1–8)*

Journal

As you read today's devotional introducing the idea of release, what situation, person, or idea was placed on your mind and heart? What would it look like to release that situation, person, or idea to Jesus? If you're hesitant or resistant, why do you think that is? Use the space below to journal your answers.

_____

_____

_____

_____

_____

_____

_____

_____

_____

_____

_____

_____

_____

Day 2

I am the true vine.

—John 15:1

For years, I had looked to success for my identity. If I was succeeding, I felt secure. If I was accomplishing something, I felt valuable. But when I failed, when I dropped the ball, or when I couldn't keep up with my self-imposed expectations, I felt like I had nothing to stand on. My sense of worth crumbled.

I saw this play out most clearly when I transitioned from being a public-school teacher to becoming the primary parent at home. Right after my daughter was born, I quit my job to homeschool my two boys, while also nursing a newborn around the clock. I hadn't anticipated how this season would stretch me. Teaching in a classroom had given me a clear sense of achievement. I could measure my success through lesson plans, student progress, and structured goals. But at home? There were no performance reviews. No data charts showing growth. Just messy days filled with phonics lessons, toddler tantrums, and exhaustion.

Many times, I ended the day feeling like my kids had taken everything out of me. I felt like a failure more often than not, questioning whether I was doing enough, being enough, or if I had made the right decision at all. My identity had been so entangled in being a teacher that when I no longer held that title, I wasn't sure who I was anymore.

That's how false vines work. They give us just enough to make us think they'll sustain us, but they can't hold us when life shakes us. They wither under pressure. They leave us feeling empty. And yet we cling to them. Because they feel familiar. Because we're afraid of what will happen if we let them go. Because in some way, we've convinced ourselves that we need them. But in the end, they cannot give us the nourishment we need to survive.

But Jesus tells us that He is the true vine.

The disciples would have recognized this imagery immediately. In the Old Testament, Israel was often referred to as God's vine, planted to bear fruit for His glory (Psalm 80:8–16; Isaiah 5:1–7). But Israel failed in this role. Time after time, the Israelites turned away from God, drawn to idols, false promises, and the ways of the world around them. The result was fruit spoiled by idolatry, injustice, and rebellion.

Like the Israelites, we often attach ourselves to things that promise life but leave us empty. We root our identity in our accomplishments, our influence, or even our ability to "get things right." We expect these things to sustain us, but false vines can't nourish us. They can only leave us depleted.

Jesus, the true vine, is different. His life never runs dry. His love never fails. His strength is never insufficient. In this verse, Jesus is saying, "I am the fulfillment of everything Israel was meant to be. Where the old vine failed, I will not. I am the true, unchanging, life-giving source."

He is calling us into something better: A connection that never dries up. A love that never wavers. A source of life that never fails. But to be nourished fully by Jesus, we have to release the things we've been drawing from that were never meant to sustain us.

When we release our grip on the things that were never meant to hold us, we finally make room for the One who can.

What are you connected to? Not just on the surface but at the deepest level of your heart. If you cling to relationships, believing that being loved by the right people will make you whole, then release and know the true vine makes you whole. If you look to success, convinced that if you achieve enough, you'll finally *be* enough, then release and know you are worthy because you are connected to Jesus. If you hold on to comfort, trying to avoid anything that feels too hard, too uncertain, too beyond your control, then release and know that He can carry your emotional burdens and is sovereign over all the areas of your life.

So much of our struggle to release comes down to fear. We've held on to these false vines—success, identity, control—not just because they promised us something but because they *became* something. They became safety nets. Our sense of value. Our proof that we mattered.

But the truth Jesus offers in John 15:1 is simple and stunning: *You don't need those things to live. You just need Me.*

He isn't one vine among many. He is *the* Vine. The only one who won't drain you dry. The only source who can truly sustain. And the invitation is open: *Let go. Connect to Me instead.*

Letting go may feel like loss, but it's actually where life begins. Because when we release our grip on the things that were never meant to hold us, we finally make room for the One who can. We begin to live—not toiling or performing but abiding. And when we abide in the true vine, we're not just surviving anymore. We're growing, resting, then becoming exactly who He created us to be.

Reflection Questions

1. What false vines have you been connected to—things you've relied on for identity, security, or meaning?

2. How has holding on to those things affected your ability to fully trust Jesus as the true vine?

3. What would it look like for you to release a false vine today and abide in Christ instead?

Day 3

My Father is the gardener. Every branch in me
that does not produce fruit he removes,
and he prunes every branch that produces
fruit so it will produce more fruit.
—John 15:1–2

love planning events. Growing up, I had dreams of becoming an associated student body (ASB) director at the school where I would eventually teach. For those of you who don't speak school acronym, ASB is the magical team that puts together the school dances, rallies, lunchtime shenanigans, and all those other moments that give high schoolers something to talk about at reunions.

Planning is my happy place, especially when it comes to holiday celebrations and birthdays. I'm the one who coordinates the perfect party and obsesses over every last detail, from the invitations to the color of the napkins. I'm also the person who finds it nearly impossible to attend an event without somehow sneaking into the planning process. I like being in the mix, okay? It's kind of my thing.

A couple of years ago, though, my girlfriends asked what I wanted to do for my birthday. Since life was hectic at the time, I said, "Nothing." Well, they knew me better than that. They sensed the unspoken desire for some form of celebration (because let's be honest, I didn't want to let my birthday go by unnoticed), and they started planning a surprise party.

Now, here's where things got tricky . . . I found out about the surprise. I know, I know, it would have been great if I had stayed blissfully unaware, but alas. And the moment I knew about it? Oh, I wanted to jump in and help! I mean, how could I not? It was practically torture to sit back and do nothing. But, friend, I am proud to report that I managed to stay out of it completely. No suggestions, no color scheme ideas, no detailed itineraries. I just let go. (And by "let go," I mean I clenched my fists and whispered "You can do this" to myself a few times.)

And you know what? It was perfect. I showed up to the most beautiful beach picnic—yummy treats, amazing company, and all the little details that made me feel so loved. My friends had thought of everything, and I got to experience the sweet joy of just being fully present without the weight of planning on my shoulders. It was such a precious time, and I have to admit, maybe not being in control once in a while has its perks!

Letting go like that isn't easy for me. If you're anything like me, you might feel the constant urge to be involved, to "make sure things get done right" or to control the process. But when it comes to our spiritual lives, that's not our job.

In John 15:2, Jesus gives us this beautiful reminder that God is the gardener of our souls and *He* is the one doing all the work. Just like I had to step back and let my friends plan the perfect birthday celebration for me, we have to step back and let God be the one to prune and shape in our lives. The branches—that's us—aren't expected to prune themselves. Our job is not to control the growth or outcomes. It's not up to us to decide what needs to stay or what needs to go. The Gardener knows what He's doing, and our role is simply to remain connected to Jesus—the true vine—and trust that God is taking care of the rest.

If God is pruning you, it's not punishment.
Rather, it's proof He sees your purpose and is
preparing you to bear even more fruit.

In the same way a gardener carefully prunes and nurtures plants, God carefully tends to us. And just like pruning a real plant can be painful (think about those sharp shears!), God's pruning in our lives can be uncomfortable too. Sometimes He removes things we thought were good for us or He cuts back areas where we felt productive.

The idea of something being cut away feels a little scary, naturally. But pruning is a sign of growth. Gardeners don't prune a dead or useless branch; they prune a healthy one to make it even more fruit-ful. So, if you feel like God is pruning certain areas of your life right now, it's not a punishment—it's because He sees more potential in you, more fruit He wants to bring out.

Let me say that again. If God is pruning you, it's not punishment. Rather, it's proof He sees your purpose and is preparing you to bear even more fruit. His pruning process might look like letting go of certain habits, mindsets, or even relationships that aren't aligned with His best for you. It might involve walking through challenging seasons that feel like a setback, but they're actually setting you up for more growth. He's positioning you for a harvest.

What exactly is the fruit, though? Is Jesus talking about achievements or success? Not exactly. Jesus is referring to spiritual fruit. It's about what's happening on the inside: the transformation of your character. Paul beautifully outlines this fruit of the Spirit in Galatians 5:22–23:

> The fruit of the Spirit is love, joy, peace, patience, kindness, goodness, faithfulness, gentleness, and self-control.

This is the kind of fruit God is producing in you as He prunes and shapes you. It's not about being busier or doing more. It's about becoming more like Jesus! As you release your grip on control and lean into His process, His Spirit works in you, transforming your heart and helping you reflect more of His character.

So take heart, friend. You don't have to hold the shears. You don't have to fight to keep what God is gently asking you to let go of. The

Gardener sees every branch, every bud, every hidden part of your heart. And when He prunes, He does it with love. Release the need to control the process. Release the fear of what might be cut away. Trust that in His hands, nothing is wasted and everything surrendered is making room for something far more fruitful.

Reflection Questions

1. How do you respond to the idea of God as the gardener who tends to your life? Do you trust Him with that role?

2. When have you experienced God's pruning in the past, and what fruit eventually came from that season?

3. What would it look like to release control today and trust God's process?

Day 4

You are already clean because of the word
I have spoken to you.
—John 15:3

Can I be real with you? When I first read John 15:3, it didn't
quite hit me. Jesus said, "You are already clean," and I wondered how that fit into the whole vine-and-branches metaphor. What did He mean, and why does this matter in the bigger
picture of staying connected to Him?

After digging deeper, I realized this verse is much more profound
than I initially thought. To understand its full significance, we need
to connect it to a scene from John 13, when Jesus washes His disciples' feet—a humble act with deep spiritual meaning.

In Jesus's time, foot washing was a practical, everyday task. You
could be freshly bathed, but after a short walk, your feet would pick
up dust from the road. You weren't dirty all over, but your feet
needed a little attention. In John 13, during Jesus's final meal with

the disciples, He took the posture of servant and began washing each of their feet, an act so unexpected that Peter at first resisted. But Jesus told him, "If I don't wash you, you have no part with me" (verse 8). It wasn't just about physical dirt; it was about spiritual readiness and relational intimacy.

Jesus used this simple act as a spiritual lesson. In our lives, we naturally pick up a little dust as we walk through the world—a stressful day at work, a tough conversation, a moment of frustration. It's important to recognize how the dust we pick up as we walk through life can gradually lead to sin if left unchecked. The small things we experience, like stress, comparison, and overcommitment, may not be sinful in themselves, but over time, they can shape our thoughts, actions, and attitudes in ways that pull us away from God. It's not that we're deeply flawed, but we accumulate life's messes. And like the disciples' feet after a long day, we need a refreshing wash.

But what if it's been a while since you've let Jesus wash the dust from your soul? Since you've cracked open the spine of your Bible and dipped into the cool waters of His Word? Since you've prayed to Jesus and let Him rinse away the grime from your heart? Should you clean up first?

I could be wrong, but I'm going to guess you probably feel the need to tidy up before letting anyone into your house. Before I have people over, I'm running around as this plays on repeat in my head: *Wait, let me just fix this real quick!* There's a bra hanging on a doorknob, crumbs left on the table from breakfast and it's dinnertime, and a trail of schoolwork left behind from our homeschool day. It's not that my house is dirty—it's just a bit disorganized, and I feel like everything has to be just right before I let someone in.

Likewise, many of us approach our spiritual lives like Peter when Jesus knelt to wash his feet. We resist the idea of letting Jesus do the work for us. We think that we should be the ones scrubbing away at this mess or that we need to clean up our act before we can let Jesus in. Here's the beautiful part: Jesus has already done the hard work of making us clean.

When He told the disciples in John 15:3, "You are already clean," He wasn't giving them a task. He was giving them freedom. He was saying, "Release the pressure. Let go of the belief that you have to make yourself presentable before coming to Me." They didn't have to work for this connection. They already had it. The deep cleansing of their soul? Done. The disciples' only job was to remain in Jesus, to trust that His work was enough, and let go of anything keeping them from resting in that truth.

The same is true for us. Jesus isn't waiting for us to dust off our spiritual lives or put everything back in its place before we come to Him. He's not sitting there with a checklist, making sure we're spotless before we can be connected to Him. In fact, He has said the exact opposite: "You are already clean." The deep, transformative work is done.

I want you to sit with this truth: *You are already clean.* There's no need to fix yourself before you can come to Jesus. He has already done the work in your heart. The connection to the Vine—to Jesus—is what allows you to experience the continual cleansing and refreshing His presence brings.

Life can be overwhelming, filling our hearts and minds with the weight of stress, unmet expectations, and all the hard things that add up over the years. But Jesus isn't asking us to carry that weight or figure it out on our own. He invites us to release it. To lay it down. To let Him wash away the dust. To simply rest in Him. No matter how dusty life gets, His Word is always there to renew, refresh, and remind us that His love is steady, His grace is sufficient, and His peace is ours to receive.

His grace covers you, His love sustains you, and His presence is enough.

Release the pressure to have it all together. You don't have to earn your place with Jesus or prove yourself worthy. He's already called you His own. Release the voice that says you must fix yourself first. Instead, step into the rest He freely offers and allow Him to refresh your soul. His grace covers you, His love sustains you, and His presence is enough.

Reflection Questions

1. In which areas of your life do you feel like you have to work harder to be "good enough" for God?

2. How does knowing that Jesus has already made you clean challenge the way you think about your spiritual growth?

3. What is one area in which you need to release the pressure to earn what has already been given freely?

Day 5

Remain in me, and I in you. Just as a branch
is unable to produce fruit by itself unless it
remains on the vine, neither can you
unless you remain in me.

—John 15:4

Up until this point, Jesus has painted the picture of the vine and the branches. He's defined the roles of the Vine and the Gardener, alluded to us as the branches, and reminded us that we are clean because of Him. But in today's verse, Jesus invites us to take action—by remaining in Him.

We're so used to juggling life, work, family, and a million other things, right? And in the middle of all that, Jesus is telling us to do something else? Yes, but this command isn't about adding one more task to our to-do list. He isn't asking us to be the gardener or even worry about how fruitful we are. This command is about simplifying. He's asking us to do one thing: *Remain.*

Let's geek out for a minute, because Jesus knew what He was talking about when He gave us this vine-and-branches metaphor. A branch can't survive on its own. It relies completely on the vine to transport life-giving water and nutrients through a system called the xylem (think: one-way superhighway from root to branch). Cut off a branch and it's game over—no water, no nutrients, no life.

And while the phloem system carries sugars produced by the leaves to other parts of the plant, even that doesn't flip the script, because the branch can only produce *if it stays connected to the vine.* The leaves don't sustain the vine; the vine sustains the whole plant. Jesus doesn't need us to survive, but He invites us to stay close, to draw everything we need from Him. Jesus, our *Living Water,* is the source of real nourishment and lasting growth.

That's why staying connected to Him matters so much. When we try to live disconnected from Jesus, the fruit of the Spirit simply doesn't grow: love, joy, peace, patience, kindness, goodness, faithfulness, gentleness, and self-control (Galatians 5:22–23). Trust me, I've tried, and it looks a lot like stress, burnout, and a whole lot of *Why is this so hard?*[*] Fruit doesn't come from hustling, no matter what hustle culture tells us. The fruit of the Spirit isn't something we can force. It grows naturally when we're rooted in Jesus.

But to get the spiritual nourishment we need to thrive, not just survive, we can't just visit Him. Visiting is what we do when we stop by someone's house for a chat or a quick coffee. Jesus wants more.

---

*The connection to Jesus doesn't mean life is no longer hard. Check out verses such as Matthew 11:28–30 and 2 Corinthians 12:9–10.

The word *remain* (or *abide* in other translations) comes from the Greek word *menó*,* which means "to dwell, to stay"—to make our home. Jesus is calling us to dwell in Him and not just check in when we're in trouble. He wants us to unpack our bags and stay for the long haul. He is asking us to make our home in Him, to stay connected, day in and day out, through the highs and lows.

There was a season when my family of six had to sell our 2,200-square-foot home. For five years, I had poured love into that home. Carefully choosing the furniture, painting the walls, making it a space where my family felt safe, comfortable, and at peace. But suddenly, all of that was behind me, and I found myself in a 1,200-square-foot rental that didn't quite feel like mine. I missed the way the light poured into the kitchen in the morning and the memories tied to each carefully chosen detail of our old house.

However, if I wanted this rental to truly feel like home, I had to do something important: release what was and embrace what could be. I had to let go of my attachment to the past and choose to invest in where I was now. I had to accept that home wasn't about square footage or familiarity; it was about presence, love, and the willingness to remain, even when things felt unfamiliar.

And isn't that what Jesus calls us to do?

To remain in Jesus is to move in with Him. Not as a guest but as someone who belongs. It means releasing our grip on the home we've built for ourselves—the place where our comfort, indepen-

---

Greek Lexicon: "3306.menó," Bible Hub, https://biblehub.com/greek/3306.htm.

dence, and self-sufficiency have been our foundation—and stepping fully into His. He welcomes us in, not as guests but as family. His presence becomes our safe space, His truth the walls that protect us, and His love the warmth that fills every room.

And here's where it gets even more beautiful: As we remain in Him, He resides in us. We hand over the keys, and He goes to work, remodeling our hearts. He rearranges the furniture, making space for peace where anxiety used to sit. He repaints the walls, covering the stains of shame and replacing them with the color of grace. He clears out the clutter of striving, comparison, and fear, making room for rest, joy, and trust. He invests in us. He makes us into a home.

He's inviting us to hand Him the blueprints and let Him build something better than we ever could.

But for this transformation to happen, we must release. We must let go of the idea that we have to manage everything ourselves. We must surrender the fear that if we don't stay in control, everything will fall apart. Jesus isn't asking us to be the architect of our own lives. He's inviting us to hand Him the blueprints and let Him build something better than we ever could.

So, the question is: Are we just visiting Jesus, or are we moving in?

Are we holding on to our own plans, or are we handing over the keys and letting Him make a home in us?

True remaining starts with release. The more we let go, the more He fills us. The more we surrender, the more He transforms us. And as we remain in Him, we don't just survive; we thrive, fully alive in the place He has prepared for us.

Reflection Questions

1. In what ways do you notice yourself treating your relationship with Jesus more like a quick visit than a dwelling place?

2. What would it look like for you to unpack and stay, building your life in God's presence rather than checking in occasionally?

3. What distractions or habits might you need to release in order to make your home in Him?

Day 6

I am the vine; you are the branches.
The one who remains in me and I in him
produces much fruit, because you can
do nothing without me.

—John 15:5

What a beautiful gift it is in a relationship to be told exactly where you stand. Until now, in this passage, we've been told who God is—the gardener. We've also been told who Jesus is—the vine. But it's not until verse 5 that we're told exactly who we are: "You are the branches."

This is our You Are Here sign on the map. And because we know where we are, we can release the roles we were never meant to carry. We are not the Gardener, responsible for orchestrating growth. We are not the Vine, the source of life itself. We are simply branches, fully dependent on Jesus for life, growth, and fruitfulness.

Remembering to be a branch is hard. We get impatient with the process. We want to see immediate results, measurable growth, and undeniable proof that we're producing something worthwhile. We assume that if we just work harder, pray more, or force the right conditions, then the fruit will come. But Jesus makes it clear: Fruit isn't the result of our effort—it's the result of our connection to Him.

Let's go back to that move I mentioned earlier, the one where my family of six left our four-bedroom, three-bathroom home and moved into a much smaller three-bedroom, one-bathroom rental on a vast piece of land. This was a necessary move that my husband and I did not take lightly. I wanted to take some of the pressure off my husband and give him the peace of mind he deserves as the provider for our family. But the decision was more than that, since we needed the financial stability that a house with a smaller monthly payment provided.

At first, I tried to focus on the positives. The rental was on twenty acres of farmland, which felt like a little taste of the future we'd always dreamed of. We want land. We want chickens. We want a huge garden and space for our kids—and eventually our grandkids—to run free. So, in some ways, this move felt like a glimpse of that life.

But if I'm honest, I also expected it to come with some spiritual fruit—a sense of peace, maybe more joy, definitely a bit of patience. I thought simplifying our life would automatically produce the stillness and steadiness in my soul that I'd been craving.

The farm was an hour away from where we used to live, which meant we were far from our family, our friends, and the community we had built. At first, I thought, *It's just a drive.* But the reality hit fast. Suddenly, the support system we had always relied on wasn't easily accessible. If we wanted a date night, it wasn't as simple as dropping off the kids with family or a trusted friend. The effort it took to arrange childcare, drive back and forth, and plan everything out just didn't feel worth it. So, we just . . . stopped.

And that one-bathroom life? Whew. Let's just say, when we'd get back from eating out, it was a full-on race to the finish line. Six people, one toilet—*May the fastest (or the most desperate) win.*

I thought we were doing it to be responsible, reset financially, and make a smart move for our future. I also thought we were moving out there to get a preview of the life we wanted, to dip our toes into homesteading and country living. But God had something completely different in mind.

Instead of just giving us land to *experience,* He gave us a season of deep work. My husband and I grew closer than ever, in ways that I don't think would have happened if we had stayed in the old house. Our kids got to be bored (which, let's be real, is a lost art these days), and I watched their relationships with one another grow stronger. But maybe the most surprising part was how we grew spiritually as a family. With fewer distractions and less support from the outside, we found ourselves turning to God more intentionally. We prayed together more. We depended on Him more, not just as individuals but as a family unit. Our kids saw us asking God for peace and provision, and they joined in those moments with a kind of raw, childlike faith. We grew closer not only to one another but also to the One who was holding us all.

This move—one we wouldn't have chosen if we hadn't *needed* to—

ended up being the reset our family didn't even know we were craving. We walked away changed.

And isn't that just like God? We expect one kind of fruit, but He produces something completely different—something far better.

We expect one kind of fruit, but God produces something completely different—something far better.

We often misunderstand the gardening process, expecting to reap a harvest during a season meant for sowing. We get frustrated when we don't see growth fast enough. We wonder why things feel stagnant, why we still struggle, why our spiritual lives don't look the way we think they should. But growth isn't something we can manufacture; it's something we receive.

Jesus has already told us: "The one who remains in me and I in him produces much fruit." It's a promise, not a productivity metric. The fruit will come not because we strive, but because we stay connected.

But to experience that fruit, we have to release our expectations of what our spiritual lives should look like. We have to let go of the idea that we should be further along by now, that our journey should match someone else's, that we should already have everything figured out. We are not the gardener—God is. And He knows exactly what we need in every season.

I didn't think moving to a farm in the middle of nowhere with no cell service would be the place where God did some of His best work in our family. But that's what happens when we release our expectations and allow Him to do things in His way, in His time.

The thing about bearing fruit is that it doesn't happen overnight. You don't plant seeds today and wake up to a thriving orchard tomorrow. Growth takes time. Roots have to go deep. Branches need to be pruned.

And sometimes it takes a while to see the evidence of what God is doing.

Maybe you're in a season in which you don't see the fruit yet. You've been faithful, you've been praying, and you've been doing the right things, but it feels like nothing is happening. Trust that God is still at work. You may not see the fruit today, but that doesn't mean He isn't growing something beneath the surface.

So, here's the invitation today: Release.

Release the expectations you've placed on yourself to be more, do more, or produce more. You are in the hands of the all-loving Gardener. Release the timeline you've created in your head for when and how you think growth should happen. Remain in Jesus, and trust that the fruit will come in His timing, through His power, and in ways that will far exceed your expectations.

Because at the end of the day, we are just the branches. And that's more than enough.

Reflection Questions

1. Where in your life have you been striving to produce fruit instead of allowing it to come from your connection to Jesus?

2. How does knowing that fruitfulness is the result of abiding change the way you see your spiritual growth?

3. What is one part of your life where you can release striving to produce fruit and lean into remaining today?

Day 7

If anyone does not remain in me,
he is thrown aside like a branch and he withers.
They gather them, throw them into the fire,
and they are burned.

—John 15:6

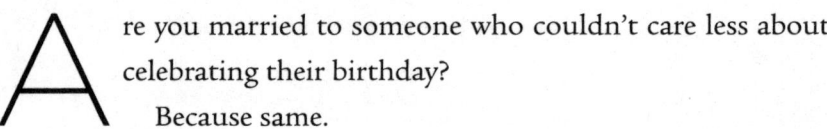re you married to someone who couldn't care less about celebrating their birthday?

Because same.

Over the years, I've tried it all for my husband's birthday. Surprise parties, weekend trips, special dinners—you name it, I've planned it. And every single time, I ended up feeling a little defeated. Not because he didn't appreciate the effort, but because deep down he genuinely didn't want to celebrate and I just could not accept that.

Then one year, he caught me off guard.

In 2021, his birthday and Mother's Day happened to fall on the same weekend—his birthday on Saturday, Mother's Day on Sunday. He told me he wanted to celebrate by going to Maui alone.

At first, I suggested, "Why don't we make it a combo trip?" I mean, it was his birthday and Mother's Day, after all. Selfishly, I didn't want to miss out on a trip to Maui, but part of me also knew that something deeper was going on between us. We weren't in the best place in our marriage. There was a disconnection we hadn't fully dealt with yet. We were in therapy, trying to work through it, but the space between us felt heavy.

Still, I invited myself along. After some consideration, prayer, and probably more therapy sessions than either of us cared to count, he agreed.

Even after he said yes, I started to second-guess going. Maybe I should let him go alone. Maybe he needed time and space more than he needed me hovering nearby. The closer we got to the trip, the more I wrestled with it.

But I ended up going anyway. And honestly? I'm so glad I did. Because while that trip didn't magically fix everything, it did remind us why we chose each other. It gave us the space to slow down, to laugh again, to simply *be* together without the noise of everyday life. It wasn't about solving all our problems. It was about choosing to stay connected when it would have been easier to pull away.

As I read John 15:6, I can't help but think how that decision to choose connection with my husband speaks to what Jesus is urging us to understand—that remaining isn't passive. It's an active, intentional choice to stay close, even when we feel inclined to withdraw.

This verse is jarring. It's one of those passages where Jesus stops us in our tracks: "If anyone does not remain in me, he is thrown aside like a branch and he withers."

It's a warning. But it's also an invitation. Jesus is saying, "Don't drift. Don't disconnect. Stay with Me."

Remaining is an active, intentional choice to stay close, even when we feel inclined to withdraw.

Because disconnection doesn't always happen in big, dramatic moments. It often happens slowly, quietly. Sometimes it looks like spiritual apathy. Sometimes it's bitterness, busyness, or distraction. Sometimes it's hurt or disappointment we haven't brought to Him.

And when we allow that space to grow between us and Jesus, we begin to wither.

I'm no expert gardener, but I do love my houseplants. And one thing I've learned? There's a difference between a plant that needs water and a plant that's too far gone. Some just need a little love and sunlight to bounce back. But others? They've gone so long without water, the life once flowing through them is hard to find, and they need more than a quick fix. They need reconnection. They've been disconnected from their source for too long. The soil's dry, the roots are brittle, and the life is gone.

That's what Jesus is saying here, not to scare us but to wake us up.

Because the moment we start thinking we can survive spiritually without Him is the moment we start to dry out. We may not notice it at first. But our peace, joy, and patience start to fade. Our love grows cold. Our spiritual rhythm starts to feel like a routine, not a relationship. And we wonder why we feel so empty.

The psalmist said the one who delights in the Lord "is like a tree planted beside flowing streams that bears its fruit in its season, and its leaf does not wither" (Psalm 1:3). And in Jeremiah, we see the same image: "He will be like a tree planted by water: it sends its roots out toward a stream, it doesn't fear when heat comes, and its foliage remains green" (17:8).

Connection to the Source is everything.

But remaining in Jesus isn't just about loving Him. Staying connected to Him is about releasing the things that are pulling you away from the Vine. It's about letting go of what competes for your heart.

Release the pride that keeps you from admitting you need Him.

Release the lies that say you're fine without a real connection.

Release the fear that if you draw near, He might not meet you there.

Release the habit of showing up in body but not in spirit.

Release the version of your faith that's more performance than presence.

Because what Jesus says next is sobering: "They gather them, throw them into the fire, and they are burned." This isn't about a struggling branch—it's about a branch that's refused connection for so long that it's no longer alive. That's the cost of not remaining. That's what Jesus *doesn't* want for you.

The fire isn't a scare tactic. It's a picture of finality. And the beauty is, you're not there. You're here. You're reading this. You're still drawing from the Vine.

Today's release isn't about shame but surrender. Let go of the things that are hardening your heart toward Jesus. Fight for your connection with Him. Draw near. Stay close. Choose again to remain. Because life is in the Vine and you were made for fruitfulness, not fire.

Reflection Questions

1. What parts of your life feel spiritually dry or disconnected? Could this be a sign of not remaining?

2. Why do you think we resist full dependence on Jesus? What fears or doubts hold you back?

3. What practices or choices help you remain connected to Jesus, not just occasionally but daily? How can you lean into those more intentionally this week?

Day 8

If you remain in me and my words remain
in you, ask whatever you want and
it will be done for you.

—John 15:7

love math. If you don't love math, hang with me for a second! I
promise, this isn't just for math people. There's something in this
verse that we can understand more deeply by using just a little bit
of math.

I have a bachelor's degree in mathematics and taught math for
seven years before becoming a homeschooling mom. Y'all, I cannot
help it when the math geek comes out in me, and often I don't know
when it's going to happen. As I read verse 7, I immediately think of
if-then clauses, also referred to as conditional statements. They're
used in mathematical proofs or to solve equations. They're pretty
straightforward: If this is true, then I can conclude that. It's all
about using the information you're given to draw a solid conclu-

sion. Well, let me tell you, John 15:7 is giving some very conditional vibes:

> *If* you remain in me and my words remain in you, [*then*] ask whatever you want and it will be done for you.

Jesus is laying down one of those if-then clauses, but we can't skip to the then without addressing the if. And too often, we do.

We want to jump straight to the promise—the "whatever you want will be done for you" part. We read this verse and think, *Okay, Jesus, I'll stay connected . . . but let's talk about the asking part!* But Jesus is showing us that our ability to ask is directly linked to our ability to remain, and not just remain in Him but let *His words remain in us.*

Abiding in Jesus and making space for His words to dwell in us are two different statements. The second part is easy to overlook but matters just as much. Because when we allow His words to take root and grow deep in our hearts, then they begin to shape how we think, speak, and live.

There are days when I wake up and immediately feel bombarded by noise. The kids are loud, the to-do list is long, and my phone starts buzzing with notifications. Before I know it, I'm scrolling through Instagram, answering emails, and singing a song I don't even like but that's stuck in my head because my kids discovered a new YouTube channel and, well, here we are. (Any other moms out there feel me on this one?)

But here's the thing: Just like that theme song got stuck in my head because I heard it over and over again, the same is true for

Jesus's words. The more I hear them, speak them, memorize them, reflect on them—the words stick. They remain.

Romans 10:17 tells us that "faith comes from what is heard, and what is heard comes through the message about Christ." If we want Jesus's words to remain in us, we have to make intentional choices to hear them. And I don't mean simply hearing them through someone else's Instagram post or a podcast, although those things are helpful. I'm talking about hearing them directly from the Source, through personal time in His Word.

There's nothing like sitting
with the Word of God for ourselves—
soaking it in, letting it transform
us from the inside out.

We live in a world where Bible-related content is everywhere. We can consume sermons, listen to Christian influencers, and read devotionals (*hello!*). And while those things are great, there's nothing like sitting with the Word of God for ourselves—soaking it in, letting it transform us from the inside out.

Deuteronomy 6:6–7 says, "These words that I am giving you today are to be in your heart. Repeat them to your children. Talk about them when you sit in your house and when you walk along the road, when you lie down and when you get up." God's Word was never meant to be something we visit occasionally. It's meant to live with us—to be repeated, remembered, recited. When it remains in us, it doesn't just stay—it shapes. It begins to rewire the way we think. It helps us discern what's true when the world is loud and confusing. And eventually, God's words are what will rise up when we pray, reflecting His heart, not just our hopes.

Jesus's promise in John 15:7 is real, but it's conditional. Before we can ask for what we want, we must remain. And before we can remain, we must release the distractions that drown out His words. Because they won't remain in us if we don't make space for them by releasing something else.

What's taking up space in your heart and mind that could be filled with His Word? Is it the noise of social media? The pressure to keep up? The opinions of others? Is it the voice in your head that always has something to prove?

Whatever it is, release it. Clear out the space. Quiet the noise.

Because when we make room for His words, they don't just stay with us—they shape us. And when they shape us, our desires align with His. And that's when we can truly ask not just for what we want but for what He wants for us.

Reflection Questions

1. What is currently filling your mind and heart, crowding out the words of Jesus?

2. How can you make space for His words to remain in you instead of allowing them to be drowned out by distractions?

3. What is one thing you can release today to make room for the voice of God in your life?

Day 9

If you remain in me and my words
remain in you, ask whatever you want
and it will be done for you.

—John 15:7

A t first glance, the second half of this verse sounds like Jesus is handing us a blank check: "[Then] ask *whatever* you want and it will be done for you." Okay, let's go!

I want the ten-acre farm with the mid-century modern barndominium—big windows, a wraparound porch, and a sunroom where I can sit and sip tea while watching my kids play outside. I want five bedrooms, and let's add a schoolroom, a craft room, two offices, and a production space so my husband can work from home. While we're at it, can we get a tennis court that doubles as a basketball court and—if possible—a hockey rink? Just putting it out there, Lord.

I'm joking (kind of), but when we first read this verse, it's easy to think it means we can ask for anything and expect to receive it. Dream house? Done. Promotion? Done. Dream vacation? Just ask.

But we know it's not that simple.

Jesus isn't just talking about asking for whatever crosses our minds; He's talking about what happens when we remain in Him. When we're truly connected to Jesus—when His words remain in us—our desires begin to shift. We still ask God for things, but our requests aren't just about us anymore. Instead of asking God to give us *what we want*, our hearts start to pray, *God, align my heart with what* You *want*.

And that's where release comes in.

Remaining in Jesus requires us to let go of our self-focused tendencies, so we can fully embrace His desires. It's not about losing who we are; rather, it's about releasing the parts of us that are chasing the wrong things. To do so, we have to take an honest look at how and why we approach God.

When we pray, are we just checking off a spiritual to-do list or are we genuinely seeking His heart? Are we going to Him only for what He can give us, or are we desiring simply to be with Him? Do our prayers focus solely on our own comfort, or do they reflect a heart that seeks His kingdom?

Now, let me be clear: Jesus is still inviting us to ask because He cares about every detail of our lives. He's not saying, "Stop bringing your desires to Me." But we need to remember that God is not transactional. He's not a vending machine. He is a Father who invites us into relationship. So in this verse, Jesus is saying, "Bring your desires to Me, and let Me refine them."

The more we remain in Him, the more we learn to desire His presence over His provisions, His heart over His hand. And as our prayers begin to reflect that, we find ourselves asking not just for what we want but also for what He wants for us. We begin to pray in ways that influence others and glorify Him.

While we know God encourages us to ask with confidence (1 John 5:14), sometimes we hesitate to pray boldly because we're afraid of disappointment. What if God doesn't answer the way we hope? What if He says no? But remaining in Him means trusting that even a seemingly unanswered prayer is actually an answered prayer. His no is just as loving as His yes because He sees what we cannot. When we truly believe He is sovereign, we can release our fear of disappointment and trust that His will, no matter what it looks like, is always for our good.

When we truly believe He is sovereign, we can release our fear of disappointment.

Now, I won't lie—releasing the fear of disappointment and choosing to trust God's no don't happen overnight. Some things, like praying for a friend's health, are easy to utter. Whereas other prayers, like asking for a grateful heart when your world is crashing down, are often difficult to speak. But transformation isn't about trying harder—it's about remaining longer. The more time we spend in His presence, the more our minds are renewed. The more we release, the more room He has to shape our desires. And before we know it, what we want is exactly what He wants for us.

So what should we be asking for?

When we've released control and are truly remaining in Him, we start asking for the things that matter most. More patience. More grace. More wisdom for the hard situations. More opportunities to love people well. Our prayers become less about getting and more about becoming.

So, here's the real question: What desires are you still holding on to that need to be surrendered? Are you clinging to a version of your life that God is asking you to release? Are you afraid to trust that His desires for you are better than your own? Are you hesitant to let go of self-focused prayers because you're not sure what He'll replace them with?

Release it.

Because when we truly release, God doesn't just take things away—He replaces them with something better. And when we remain in Him, we don't just get what we want; we start wanting what He gives.

Reflection Questions

1. When you think about what you've asked God for recently, have your prayers reflected His will or your own desires?

2. How can remaining in Jesus transform both the way you pray and what you ask for?

3. What is one prayer you need to release today, trusting that God's way is better?

Day 10

My Father is glorified by this:
that you produce much fruit and
prove to be my disciples.
—John 15:8

The idea of bringing God glory can feel a bit lofty, right? Like, how can I, a regular, flawed person, bring honor and praise to the Creator of the universe—a set-apart, perfect being? Isaiah 43:6–7 confirms that from the beginning, God designed us to glorify Him: "Bring my sons from far away, and my daughters from the ends of the earth—everyone who bears my name and is created for my glory. I have formed them; indeed, I have made them." So even as imperfect beings, we can bring God glory. But how? What specifically glorifies God?

Jesus spelled it out in John 15:8. We glorify the Father when we bear much fruit and live as His disciples. Remember, the fruit that glorifies God isn't something we produce by sheer willpower. It's not about striving harder, doing more, or proving our worth. Jesus is clear: We are branches, not the Vine. The fruit comes from remaining connected to Him, and remaining isn't just about connection—it's also about letting go.

Too often, we place unnecessary pressure on ourselves to be "good Christians" who bear fruit through our own effort. We measure our worth by what we can accomplish, how well we behave, or how much impact we have. But glorifying God isn't about striving—it's about surrender.

Glorifying God isn't about striving— it's about surrender.

We don't bear fruit because we try harder. We bear fruit because we let go.

We release the pressure to perform, trusting that abiding in Jesus is enough. We release self-reliance, remembering that apart from Him, we can do nothing (John 15:5). We release the fear of pruning, knowing that when the Father removes what no longer serves us, it's for our good.

God is glorified when His work is evident in us. Not when we're out here trying to manufacture growth but when our lives reflect something we could never produce on our own.

Think about a tree that produces abundant fruit. Who gets the credit—the tree or the gardener?

A tree doesn't stress about fruitfulness. It doesn't strive, hustle, or force itself to grow. It simply remains planted, receives what it needs, and allows the process to happen. The gardener, however, is the one who nurtures, prunes, and ensures that fruit comes in its season.

The same is true for us. When we release the pressure to "prove" our faith and instead trust the Gardener, our lives begin to produce evidence of His work. Love, joy, peace, patience—these aren't accomplishments to strive for. They are the natural consequences of abiding in Him. And when that fruit appears, it's clear that God is the one who made it happen.

We know that when we remain in Jesus, our lives begin to bear fruit, not because of anything we force but because of what He produces in us. And when that fruit appears, it's undeniable.

Have you ever met someone and immediately thought, *There's something different about them*? I know someone like that. The moment she walks into a room, the atmosphere shifts. There's a joy about her that isn't circumstantial, a peace that is unshaken, and a wisdom that feels weighty, yet full of grace. When she speaks, she speaks with such truth and kindness that you can't help but lean in. She doesn't strive to be noticed, but she carries a light that draws people in—a light that is nothing but the radiance of Jesus.

She's not producing this fruit by trying harder. She's simply abiding. She has released self-reliance and surrendered her plans to the Gardener, and she trusts Him to prune what needs to go. Because she has let go of everything that hinders fruitfulness, what remains is pure, undeniable evidence of God's glory.

And that's the point. When we release, remain, and bear fruit, it's not us who people see—it's Him.

Something incredible happens when we release the burden of trying to "be fruitful" on our own. Instead of constantly evaluating ourselves—*Am I growing? Am I doing enough?*—we experience freedom in simply being with Jesus.

And here's the beautiful part: The fruit still comes. Not through striving but through surrender. Not through force but through faithfulness.

And when that fruit shows up in our lives—when others see a peace that surpasses understanding (Philippians 4:7), a joy that isn't dependent on circumstances, a love that isn't conditional—it's not us they see. It's Him.

That is how we glorify the Father.

Reflection Questions

1. How does knowing that your fruitfulness brings God joy change the way you see your spiritual walk?

2. Where in your life have you been holding on to your own vision of success rather than trusting God's plan?

3. What step can you take today to release your plans and let God be glorified in your life?

Rest

Day 11

The other night, I collapsed into bed after a long day, ready to finally rest. I had been running all day—making meals, cleaning up messes, prepping lessons, teaching lessons, handling work, checking things off my list. I was physically exhausted. But as soon as my head hit the pillow, my mind kept going. *Did I respond to that message? Am I doing enough for my kids? Should I be further along in this area of my life?* Instead of resting, I was replaying, rethinking, and trying to mentally fix everything I had already "released."

If you're anything like me, rest does not come naturally. Even when we say we've let go, there's this little voice in the back of our heads whispering, *But what happens now?* We've spent the last ten days reflecting on release, learning to let go of control, surrender burdens, and trust God. But release isn't the end of the rhythm—it's only the beginning. Up next is rest.

And this is where the tension comes in. What does real rest actually look like?

Let's be honest: Rest can be confusing. Especially when we have responsibilities. People depend on us. There are deadlines to meet, meals to cook, and always more work to do. So when Jesus invites us to rest in Him by saying, "Apart from me you can do nothing" (John 15:5, NIV), does He mean that we should just stop everything and rest? Do we wait for life to figure itself out while we sit still? That can't be what Jesus meant.

Our culture offers a lot of ideas about rest. It tells us we need a vacation, a spa day, or the perfect morning routine to truly feel at peace. And while none of those things are bad, they don't offer the kind of rest that Jesus is inviting us into. You can be sitting on a beach with a book in your hand and still be restless. Or you can be in the middle of a busy season, working hard, and still be at peace because you're resting in something greater than yourself.

Rest is not about inactivity. It's about security. It's about resting in the confidence that what you've let go of is being held by Someone far more capable. And if we're honest, that's the part we struggle with the most. Because resting requires trust.

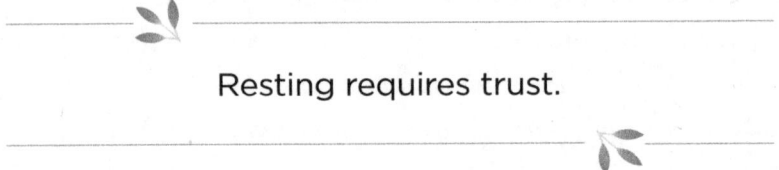

Resting requires trust.

Over the years, we've had several different nannies, and let me tell you, who I leave my kids with determines how much I can actually be at ease while I'm away. Some nannies made it easy. I'd hand over the schedule, walk out the door, and never think twice. Others? I'd be checking my phone, rushing through errands, and feeling that anxious pull to get back home as soon as possible.

I think we do the same thing with God. How much we truly rest depends on how much we trust the One we're releasing things to. If we don't fully trust His care, we'll still carry the weight of what we're supposed to be handing over.

And this is where release and rest intersect. We cannot fully rest until we trust God with what we have released into His hands. Resting in Him means we are fully present with the truth of His Word, confident that we don't have to carry what isn't ours to hold. It means believing that His ways hold us steady, while our striving only keeps us restless.

I know all this, yet my fear of what will happen if I truly release control keeps me from fully resting. I want to trust God, but I also want the inside scoop on *how* everything works out. I want to surrender, but I also want to have a backup plan just in case. But real rest doesn't work that way. We either trust God fully or we don't.

And trust is where we find rest.

So as we step into this next part of the rhythm—rest—we will continue to release. Because rest is not passive; it's a practice. It's a heart posture of believing God is who He says He is. As we release, we rest. As we rest, we release. And as we do, we begin to experience the kind of peace that comes only from remaining in Him.

Take a deep breath. Are you willing to trust God enough to truly rest?

Stay in His Love

THE INVITATION TO REST

The night is still. You're walking with Jesus, just beyond the upper room. The hush of evening wraps around you. His steps are steady beside yours, and as He speaks, there's a calm authority in His voice. He isn't in a hurry. These words—His final words before the Cross—are for you. Read these words slowly, like Jesus is speaking them directly to you. Listen closely. Let the quiet hold you as He begins.

As the Father has loved me, I have also loved you. Remain in my love. If you keep my commands you will remain in my love, just as I have kept my Father's commands and remain in his love.

I have told you these things so that my joy may be in you and your joy may be complete.

This is my command: Love one another as I have loved you. No one has greater love than this: to lay down his life for his friends. You are my friends if you do what I command you. I do not call you servants anymore, because a servant doesn't know what his master is doing. I have called you friends, because I have made known to you everything I have heard from my Father. You did not choose me, but I chose you. I appointed you to go and produce fruit and that your fruit should remain, so that whatever you ask the Father in my name, he will give you.

This is what I command you: Love one another. (John 15:9–17)

Journal

When you think about rest, what thoughts or emotions arise? Does the idea of resting in God feel freeing, difficult, or even impossible? Why do you think that is? Use the space below to journal your answers.

_____

_____

_____

_____

_____

_____

_____

_____

_____

_____

_____

_____

_____

_____

Day 12

As the Father has loved me,
I have also loved you.
—John 15:9

The other day, I was moving through my to-do list when my daughter asked me to take her braids down. I love caring for her hair, but I had too much on my plate. I told her I'd get to it later in the week.

Now, in the past, I might have tried to squeeze it in, pushing myself beyond my limits to avoid disappointing her. But in that moment, I made peace with the fact that I couldn't do everything at once. I released the need to be the one to do it all, and what happened next was a beautiful reminder that love has a way of filling the spaces we leave open.

Instead of waiting for me, she went and asked her older brother for help. And to my surprise, he said yes. There they were: she on the floor, he on the couch, carefully undoing each braid. I snapped a picture, moved by the sweetness of the moment.

Later, as I looked at that image, I realized something even deeper. My husband is the one who has always cared for everyone's hair in our home. He's done my locs, cut our sons' hair, taken down and styled our daughter's braids, and even groomed our dog. And now my son, without hesitation, was passing that love forward.

This is how love works. True love, the kind that shapes and sustains us, isn't just spoken—it's demonstrated. It's received, carried, and passed on. As a young girl, I learned the different Greek words for love at church. There's *philia,* the deep, affectionate love shared between friends. *Storge,* the natural bond of family love. *Eros,* the passionate, romantic love. And then there's *agape*—the highest, most selfless love.* *Agape* is not dependent on emotions or conditions. It's unwavering, sacrificial, and intentional. This is the love Jesus says the Father has for Him that He now extends to us. And because it is based on who He is, not what we do, we can rest in it.

That's where so many of us struggle, isn't it?

We are wired to earn, to prove, to strive. We carry this belief that love has to be worked for. That if we don't measure up, we'll lose it. But Jesus isn't just saying, "I love you." He's telling us, "I love you with the same *agape* love the Father has for Me." That means His love for us isn't based on how well we perform, how much we accomplish, or even how much faith we have on any given day.

*C. S. Lewis, *The Four Loves* (HarperOne, 2017).

It is constant. Secure. Unshakable.

Yet, instead of resting in this love, we exhaust ourselves trying to deserve it. We measure our worth by productivity. We withhold rest from ourselves because "we haven't earned it." We struggle to believe that God truly delights in us, not because of what we do but simply because we are His.

And so we resist His invitation to rest.

But Jesus didn't just talk about love. He rested in love and became love incarnate. Jesus didn't walk this earth proving His worth. He moved with confidence in the Father's love. He healed without hesitation, served without striving, and gave of Himself without fearing that He'd run empty.

We see this love in action when He touched the untouchable—the leper whose skin made him an outcast. Instead of recoiling in fear, Jesus reached out, breaking the barrier that had kept the man isolated for so long (Matthew 8:2–3).

God's love is enough.

We see it when He stopped to acknowledge the woman who had been bleeding for twelve years, even though an entire crowd was pressing against Him. He could have let her receive her healing and disappear, but instead, He turned to her, calling her His daughter (Mark 5:25–34).

We see it in the ultimate act of love: when He laid down His life on the cross. A love that bore the weight of our sin so we wouldn't have to. A love that freed us so we could walk in peace, knowing we are fully known and still fully loved.

This is the love He invites us to rest in.

Rest is a posture of the heart. It's choosing to believe God's love is enough—enough to cover our failures, enough to sustain us in our weariness, enough to hold us even when we don't feel worthy of being held.

So how do we practice this kind of rest?

- WE RELEASE THE NEED TO EARN HIS LOVE. It's already been given. Jesus said, "Come to me, all of you who are weary and burdened, and I will give you rest" (Matthew 11:28). His love isn't something to work for; it's something to receive.

- WE REMIND OURSELVES OF TRUTH. The Enemy would love for us to believe that God's love is fragile, that it can be lost with one misstep. But Romans 8:38–39 tells us that nothing—*nothing*—can separate us from His love. Not our failures, not our doubts, not our weaknesses.

- WE REFLECT HIS LOVE OUTWARD. Just like my son unknowingly mirrored his father's example, we are called to extend the love we've received (John 13:35). The more we abide in Christ, the more His love overflows into the ways we serve, encourage, and uplift those around us.

Just as my husband's love has shaped our home and now moves through our children, the Father's love moves through Jesus and is now poured into us. When we remain in that love, we don't just experience it—we reflect it. We become carriers of it, passing it on in ways we may not even realize.

So today, I invite you to release whatever is keeping you from resting in His love. Maybe it's the belief that you have to prove yourself. Maybe it's the fear that His love isn't really for you. Whatever it is, let it go. His love isn't going anywhere, and you don't have to work for what's already been freely given.

Instead, rest. Rest in a love that is unwavering. A love that is steady. A love that was always meant to hold you.

Reflection Questions

1. In what areas do you find yourself striving for love that has already been given to you?

2. How does understanding *agape* love change the way you see yourself and your relationship with God?

3. Take a moment to reflect on how Jesus has shown His love for you personally. How can you rest in that love today?

Day 13

Remain in my love. If you keep my commands
you will remain in my love, just as I have kept my
Father's commands and remain in his love.

—John 15:9-10

Before kids, before life got full and schedules got complicated, my husband and I lived in a little duplex where we had all the time in the world to be goofy with each other. We'd playfully bicker, tease, and test each other's patience just for fun—nothing serious, just the kind of lighthearted back-and-forth that comes when you're comfortable with another person.

One day, in the middle of one of those playful moments, I threw a cup at him. Not hard, not in anger, but just a playful toss, meant to keep the joke going.

But the moment the cup left my hand, I knew something was off.

His whole demeanor shifted. The laughter that had filled the space just seconds before was gone, replaced with something I didn't recognize. He looked at me, serious now, and said, "Please don't throw things at me."

At first, I was confused. It was a joke, right? It was playful, wasn't it? But as we talked, I realized it had triggered something deep, something unhealed. He opened up about childhood wounds—experiences that I had never lived but that shaped the way he moved through the world. What had felt small to me felt massive to him.

And because I loved him, because I wanted him to feel safe with me, I had to honor that.

> Boundaries are not barriers to love;
> instead, they are the very things
> that allow love to thrive.

This is what love does. It listens. It adjusts. It respects the boundaries when our loved one says, "This is where I feel safe, and this is where I don't."

And isn't this what Jesus is inviting us into? "If you keep my commands you will remain in my love, just as I have kept my Father's commands and remain in his love."

We often hear the word *commands* and immediately think of rigid rules, of obligation, of something restrictive. But what if we thought of them as boundaries? As God's way of saying, "This is where you will flourish. This is where you will find peace. This is how you remain in the love I've already poured out for you."

Boundaries are not barriers to love; instead, they are the very things that allow love to thrive. And when we honor them, we find rest.

I've learned that relationships require boundaries to be safe, and safe relationships are the ones we can rest in. Without boundaries, relationships become chaotic. Expectations become unclear. People feel unheard, unseen, and misunderstood. But when boundaries are honored—when both people agree on what love looks like and commit to staying within that space—there's peace.

God's love is no different.

The commands of Jesus are not a test we have to pass. They are not a burden placed on our backs. They are an invitation to rest in the way of love that He has already laid out for us. They help us recognize what keeps us close to Him and what pulls us away.

Think about the first and greatest commandment: "Love the Lord your God with all your heart, with all your soul, and with all your mind" (Matthew 22:37). That's a boundary. It's a call to keep God at the center of our lives, to guard our hearts from giving ultimate love and devotion to anything else. Not because God is insecure and needs our attention, but because He knows that when our love is rightly ordered, our souls are at peace.

Think about the second commandment He mentions: "Love your neighbor as yourself" (Matthew 22:39). Another boundary. A call to live in a way that honors, respects, and values the people around us—not out of obligation, but because love cannot thrive where selfishness rules.

Think about the rhythms Jesus Himself lived by. He honored the boundary of rest, pulling away from the crowds to spend time alone with the Father. He honored the boundary of truth, refusing to water down His message even when it made people uncomfortable. He honored the boundary of love, choosing to lay down His life so that we could find ours.

Boundaries are not about restriction. They are about freedom—the kind of freedom that allows love to be steady, safe, and whole.

When we live within the boundaries of God's love, we experience rest. We don't have to keep second-guessing where we stand with Him. We don't have to stay stuck in survival mode, hoping we're doing enough. We don't have to live anxiously, constantly questioning whether we're on the right path. We simply remain.

Remaining in His love is not passive. It is not standing still, waiting for something to happen. It is an active, intentional abiding. It is choosing daily to stay within the space He has made for us, to trust that His way is good, to let go of anything that pulls us away from His peace.

Just as I honored my husband's boundary because I wanted him to feel safe with me, we honor God's boundaries because we trust that He loves us.

So, what does that look like in practice?

Living within the space of His love looks like slowing down long enough to listen. To recognize when you've been running yourself ragged, pushing past the limits He's set for you. It looks like surrendering—letting go of the things that are too heavy, the expectations you were never meant to carry, the pressure to do more, be more, prove more. It looks like trust—believing that His commands are not about controlling you but about protecting you. That His love is not something you have to strive for but something you get to rest in.

Today, God invites you to rest. Rest in a love that is not demanding or exhausting. Rest in the boundaries that keep you safe. Rest in the truth that you are already held, already loved, already secure. Because when you remain in His love, you are home.

Reflection Questions

1. Think about a time when someone set a boundary with you in love. How did that boundary shape your relationship, and what did it reveal about trust and safety in that space?

2. Now think about a time when someone honored a boundary you set. How did that affect your sense of safety and trust in the relationship? How does that help you understand the connection between God's commands and His love?

3. In what areas of your life do you struggle to trust God's boundaries as a source of rest rather than restriction? How might surrendering to His way bring you deeper peace?

Day 14

I have told you these things so that
my joy may be in you and your joy
may be complete.

—John 15:11

When I was a little girl growing up in a small Baptist church, my mother's voice was a constant presence. She has a beautiful, rich tone, and you could often find her standing at the front of the church, leading the choir or singing a solo. One song she used to lead was "Praise Is What I Do." The underlying theme of the song was expressed in these words: "Through the good and the bad / I'll praise You."*

I didn't fully grasp the weight of those words back then. I just knew my mother sang them with conviction, that the melody filled

*William Murphy, "Praise Is What I Do," track 8 on *All Day*, Sony Urban/Epic, 2005.

the sanctuary, and that people in the pews would sway, eyes closed, hands lifted. But now, as a grown woman who has walked through both mountaintops and valleys, I understand them in my bones.

Because there have been days—hard days, weary days—when life felt heavy, when my heart was low, when I didn't have the words to pray. And yet, without even thinking about it, I would find myself humming an old hymn or swaying to the rhythm of a worship song.

Praising the Lord—lifting my eyes to Him, even when I didn't feel like it—has been one of the most steadying things in my life. It has carried me through seasons of grief, through uncertainty, through the moments when joy felt distant. And in those moments, I've realized something profound: Joy isn't found in our circumstances; it's found in the presence of God.

This is the joy Jesus is talking about in John 15:11. He said, "I have told you these things so that my joy may be in you and your joy may be complete." Notice He didn't just say, "So you may have joy." He said, "So that my joy may be in you." The joy He offers is His own—it's the same joy that sustained Him, the joy rooted in His relationship with the Father, the joy that remained even as He faced the Cross.

Jesus's joy wasn't about comfort or ease. It wasn't based on circumstances going His way. His joy was rooted in something deeper: the unshakable assurance that God was in control, that His purpose was secure, that He was held, even in His suffering. And that's the joy He offers us—not the fleeting kind that comes and goes with the ups and downs of life but a joy that steadies us, anchors us, and gives us rest.

One of the clearest examples of this joy in Scripture is found in Acts 16. Paul and Silas had been thrown into prison, not for doing anything wrong but for preaching the gospel. They had been beaten, shackled, and locked in the innermost cell. By all accounts, they should have been discouraged, hopeless, exhausted. And yet, in the middle of the night, instead of sinking into despair, they started singing (verse 25).

They lifted their voices in praise, filling that dark prison cell with worship. And as they did, something incredible happened: An earthquake shook the foundations of the prison, the doors flew open, and their chains fell off (verse 26).

Their circumstances hadn't changed when they started singing. The bruises on their bodies were still fresh. They were still in a cell. But their joy wasn't dependent on their situation; it was rooted in their confidence in God. Their praise wasn't just a response to freedom—it was the very thing that ushered in freedom.

And isn't that how joy works? It shifts our perspective. It lifts our eyes from what's wrong to the One who is always right. It reminds us that even in the darkest places, we are not alone.

So often, we chase happiness, mistaking it for joy. But happiness is circumstantial. It's what we feel when things are going well—when we get the job, when relationships are thriving, when life feels easy. And while happiness is a gift, it's also temporary.

Joy, on the other hand, is an internal stability in spite of external circumstances. It is, as Tony Evans says in his study Bible, "a settled assurance and quiet confidence in God's sovereignty that results in the decision to praise him.""* It's knowing that even when life is un-predictable, God is still faithful. And this kind of joy leads to rest.

Because when we trust that God is in control, we don't have to carry the weight of figuring everything out. When we are rooted in His presence, we don't have to strive for joy because it flows from Him. When we lift our voices in praise, even when life is hard, we find that joy has a way of filling the spaces we didn't even know were empty.

Joy is an internal stability in spite of external circumstances.

So how do we live this out? How do we move from striving for joy to resting in it?

First, we *root ourselves in His presence*—not just on Sundays, not just when life feels good, but in the quiet, ordinary moments of our days. In John 15, Jesus isn't just giving us a suggestion; He's giving us a road map. Remaining in Him means staying connected, allowing His love and truth to anchor us even when circumstances try to shake us.

Second, we *choose to praise Him, even when we don't feel like it.* Paul

---

*Tony Evans, *CSB Tony Evans Study Bible: Advancing God's Kingdom Agenda* (Holman, 2019), 150.

and Silas sang in a prison cell, not because they were happy about their situation, but because they knew the One who held their future. Joy is often found on the other side of worship—when we lift our eyes off our problems and onto the One who is greater.

Next, we *release the need to control everything.* How often do we tie our joy to our ability to manage outcomes? We think, *If I can just fix this, plan that, or ensure this goes my way, then I'll have peace.* But real joy—the kind that leads to rest—comes from trusting that God is sovereign. It's the quiet confidence that even when life feels uncertain, He is still in control.

And finally, we *invite joy in,* not as a fleeting emotion but as a steady foundation. This kind of joy isn't about ignoring hardship or pretending everything is okay. It's about making space for God's presence, knowing that in Him, we have something unshakable. Joy doesn't mean we never grieve, struggle, or feel disappointment; rather, it means that even in those moments, we are not without hope.

In John 15:11, Jesus didn't say, "I want you to be happy." He said, "I have told you this so that my joy may be in you and that your joy may be complete" (NIV). His joy is our resting place. His joy sustains us, carries us, and reminds us that we are held by a love that never fails.

Joy is not something to chase but something to receive and rest in. Let it meet you where you are. Let it remind you that you are not alone. Let it settle deep into your spirit, bringing the kind of peace that comes only from Him.

Reflection Questions

1. How does Jesus's definition of joy—one that remains even in suffering—challenge the way you've understood joy in your own life?

2. What are some ways you've experienced joy in God's presence, even in difficult seasons? How can you lean into that joy more intentionally?

3. Praise and joy are deeply connected. What is one way you can practice praising God this week, not just in response to good circumstances but as a way of resting in His complete joy?

Day 15

This is my command: Love one another
as I have loved you.
—John 15:12

n my last couple of years as a teacher, my life was *full*. And by full,
I mean completely overloaded.

I was up at 4 A.M., and then I'd race to get to my classroom
early because an empty campus made for productivity. Many days
I was getting to school even before the custodial and cafeteria staff.
I taught six periods a day and managed around 180 students—
grading papers, creating lesson plans, keeping up with emails, taking calls from parents, and handling the inevitable teenage drama
that came with the job. On top of that, I was the ASB director and
the Black Student Union adviser, planning events, mentoring students, and making sure everything ran smoothly.

By the time I left work, I wasn't walking to my car—I was *crawling*.
And yet, somehow, my day wasn't over.

At home, I was trying to be the present wife and mother—making dinner, doing bedtime routines, keeping up with friendships and playdates, hosting LifeGroup, where church friends came over to discuss the sermon from the week before. My friendships were suffering because I couldn't keep up with the texts or coffee dates. The Lord felt distant because by the time I sat down to read my Bible, my eyelids were already closing. And let's not forget that by my final year of teaching, I was pregnant with my third child.

I was pouring everything out. And there was nothing left to give.

I remember having a recurring conversation with my husband in that season in which he would lovingly tell me, "I feel like we're getting your leftovers."

Oof. That one stung.

Not because he said it in a hurtful way, but because he was right. My family—my greatest calling—was getting only the scraps of my energy, my patience, my love. I was loving from depletion.

I was showing up for everyone, saying yes to everything, thinking *this* was what love looked like. But Jesus doesn't ask us to love from a place of exhaustion. He asks us to love as He has loved us, and Jesus loves from *abundance, not burnout.*

Whew, girl . . . does this remind you of Mary and Martha? Because . . . same.

You probably know the story. Jesus comes to their home, and Martha is doing *the most*—running around, handling all the details, trying to make everything just right. Meanwhile, her sister, Mary, is just sitting; she's listening to Jesus and soaking up every word He says.

And Martha, bless her heart, *loses it.* She said, "Lord, don't you care that my sister has left me to serve alone? So tell her to give me a hand" (Luke 10:40).

I feel her frustration. Because when you're running yourself ragged, when you're pouring out for everyone else, it's hard not to resent the people who seem so . . . unbothered.

But Jesus? He doesn't scold Mary for sitting. Instead, He gently redirects Martha's heart:

"Martha, Martha, you are worried and upset about many things, but one thing is necessary. Mary has made the right choice, and it will not be taken away from her" (Luke 10:41–42).

Martha wasn't doing anything wrong—she was serving others! But she was serving from a place of striving instead of rest. She thought love meant doing more, but Jesus was showing her that love starts with being filled first.

And isn't that exactly what we do? We run ourselves into the ground—serving, showing up, meeting needs—until we're too exhausted to enjoy even the people we love. But Jesus is saying, "You don't have to love from depletion. Come sit with Me first."

If we're not careful, we can convince ourselves that love means self-sacrifice to the point of emptiness, that the more exhausted we are, the more loving we must be. But that's not the love Jesus demonstrated.

He took time to withdraw and pray (Luke 5:16). He made space for stillness with the Father. He rested. And because of that, when He showed up to love—whether it was healing the sick, teaching the crowds, or serving His disciples—He was fully present.

When we remain in His love, we learn to love like Him, not from striving but from the overflow of His presence.

And here's the beautiful thing: When we rest in Him, our boundaries shift naturally. We stop trying to do it *all*. We learn to say no. We release the weight of people's expectations. We start prioritizing what actually matters. Loving others as Jesus has loved us isn't about overextending ourselves; rather, it's about being so filled with Him that His love naturally flows out of us.

I look back now and realize something: When I finally started releasing the weight of doing it all, when I finally let go of the pressure to be everything for everyone, my love became more intentional. I was no longer snapping at my husband or impatient with my kids (as much, because, let's be honest, that still happens). I wasn't resenting my commitments. I started making decisions from rest, not exhaustion.

When we release what was never ours to carry, when we rest in Jesus's love first, we begin to love from a place of peace rather than pressure. And that love? That's the kind that transforms. That's the kind that endures.

Because love—real, lasting, Christlike love— was never meant to be given from depletion.

So today, before you pour out, pause. Take a moment to sit at His feet. Let His love fill you first. Because love—real, lasting, Christlike love—was never meant to be given from depletion.

Reflection Questions

1. Have you ever found yourself loving from depletion instead of abundance? What was the result?

2. How does remaining in Jesus's love help you set boundaries that allow you to love well?

3. What is one way you can intentionally sit at His feet this week, soaking in His words, before pouring into others?

Day 16

No one has greater love than this:
to lay down his life for his friends.
—John 15:13

Picture your house at its absolute worst. Dishes piled in the sink, dried food clinging to plates. Laundry baskets overflowing with unfolded clothes, some clean, some questionable. Toys scattered across the floor—Legos waiting to pierce an unsuspecting foot—and stuffed animals tossed haphazardly across the couch. Toothpaste smeared across bathroom sinks. Rings of soap scum circling the tub. Bras hanging from doorknobs. Dust thick on the shelves, laundry piled on the bed, a chaotic mess in every direction.

Now imagine something worse.

That was my house the day my husband convinced me to step away and take the kids out for a few hours. At the time, I was pregnant with my third child, teaching full-time, and already exhausted

from the constant demands of work, motherhood, and the relent-
less fatigue that comes with growing a human. My husband was
holding it down at home, juggling life with our two toddler boys
while also trying to build a business from scratch. We were both
stretched beyond our limits, and it showed.

I remember looking around that morning, feeling the weight of
all that needed to be done, but I didn't have it in me to fix it. So, we
left. I told myself I'd deal with it later.

Hours later, we walked back through the front door, and I stopped
in my tracks.

The smell of Pine-Sol and lavender hit me first. Then my eyes ad-
justed and I saw the miracle. Sparkling countertops, wiped clean of
every sticky fingerprint. Ceiling fans, dust-free and moving silently
above us. The floors, freshly vacuumed, the vacuum lines still visible
like someone had just finished. Toys, not only picked up but orga-
nized. Laundry, *folded*. Bathrooms, pristine—sinks scrubbed, mirrors
clear, toilets gleaming.

It felt like I had walked into the wrong house.

Tears welled in my eyes as I realized what had happened. While we
were out, my friends had shown up. One of them had watched everyone's kids while the others stepped into my mess—literally—and
cleaned my house from top to bottom.

It was overwhelming. Humbling. Almost too much to accept.

Because the truth is, I was struggling to let people *see* my mess, let
alone *clean* it. I was okay with sharing that I was tired, that life felt
like too much, but I hadn't expected anyone to do something about
it. And yet, they had.

As I studied John 15:13, this moment came flooding back to me.

Jesus said, "No one has greater love than this: to lay down his life for his friends."

We often associate this verse with Jesus's ultimate sacrifice on the cross, and rightfully so. But His willingness to lay Himself down wasn't just about His death. It was about how He *lived*.

Jesus continually laid Himself down for the people He loved.

He laid Himself down when He touched the leper (Matthew 8:1–3), stepping into the physical and social mess of someone others refused to go near.

He laid Himself down when He stopped for blind Bartimaeus (Mark 10:46–52), taking the time to listen and restore dignity to a man others tried to silence.

He laid Himself down when He walked miles out of His way to meet the Samaritan woman at the well (John 4:1–42), breaking cultural barriers to bring her truth, healing, and acceptance.

Again and again, Jesus moved toward people in their need. He didn't shy away from the messy, broken places. He *stepped in*.

And that's what my friends did for me that day.

They saw my exhaustion and didn't flinch. They noticed my mess and didn't judge. They didn't just say, "Let us know if you need anything." They showed up. They laid down their time, their comfort, their energy, not because they had to, but because love moves. Love sacrifices. Love steps in.

Jesus has already proven the depth of His love. If He willingly *died* for us, then why do we still struggle to trust Him with the burdens we carry? Why do we insist on holding on to things we were never meant to carry—our worries, our anxieties, our endless to-do lists—when the One who laid down His life for us is also willing to hold *everything* that weighs us down?

He doesn't flinch at the weight we carry. He doesn't stand back and wait for us to figure it out. And unlike me in the gym, struggling to check my form and readjust my stance to lift a weight I was never meant to carry, Jesus doesn't need to check His posture before He picks up our burdens. He just carries them. Effortlessly. Completely.

And yet, so often, we resist.

> The One who laid down His
> life for you is also willing to
> hold every burden, every worry,
> every ounce of exhaustion.

I resisted the love of my friends at first. I felt the urge to apologize for the mess, to downplay my exhaustion, to explain why things had gotten so bad. I felt exposed. But they weren't there to judge. They were there to love me.

Jesus does the same. He isn't waiting for you to clean up your life before you come to Him. He isn't expecting you to carry what you were never meant to hold. His love steps in, meets you where you are, and says, "You don't have to do this alone."

What would it look like for you to rest in His love? To let Jesus carry what is too heavy for you? To finally exhale, knowing you don't have to hold it all together?

Maybe it starts with admitting that you're tired. Maybe it starts with saying yes when someone offers to help. Maybe it's choosing to believe—really believe—that the One who laid down His life for you is also willing to hold every burden, every worry, every ounce of exhaustion.

Whatever it is, know this: You are not alone. Jesus has already gone before you. His love isn't passive. It moves mountains. It carries your burdens. It steps in. And because of that, you can rest.

Reflection Questions

1. Think of a time when someone demonstrated sacrificial love toward you. How did it affect you, and what did it reveal about God's love?

2. What is one area of your life in which you struggle to accept help from others? From Jesus? Why do you think that is?

3. Jesus willingly laid down His life for you. What would it look like for you to trust Him more fully with the burdens you're carrying?

Day 17

You are my friends if you do what I command you.
I do not call you servants anymore, because
a servant doesn't know what his master is doing.
I have called you friends, because I have made known
to you everything I have heard from my Father.
—John 15:14–15

Friendship is a beautiful thing, isn't it? A *true* friend is someone who knows you, sees you, and loves you anyway. A friend is someone you trust with your joy, your fears, your ugly tears, and your unfiltered thoughts. Someone who doesn't pull away when you're at your worst but leans in closer.

For a long time, I didn't know if I had that kind of friend.

After my sister-in-law passed away, I found myself standing at my kitchen sink, overwhelmed by grief. It wasn't just the grief of losing her—it was something *deeper*. It was as if decades of pain, disappointment, and loss had been silently collecting inside me, waiting for the right time to surface. And in that moment, it hit me like a tidal wave.

I didn't know what to do with it. So, I did what I'd always done: I kept moving. I kept showing up. I kept pushing through. But no amount of pushing through could silence what was rising up inside me. I knew I needed something more, so I signed up for a three-week therapy intensive with a Christian therapist, one that would take me away from my daily responsibilities and into a place of silence and solitude.

I went there with the expectation that I was going to meet with God. And I did. But not in the way I thought. I expected to pursue Him, to seek Him out, to work hard at finding Him in my stillness. But when I arrived, I realized I didn't have to do any of that. I didn't have to strive. I didn't have to earn His attention. He was already there.

It was as if He spoke gently to my heart, *Girl, I've been here.* And I finally let go.

I fell apart in a way I never had before. I wept, I grieved, I released. All the pain I had been carrying, all the pressure to keep it together—it all came undone *in His presence.*

And in that breaking, I experienced something I never had before: *rest.*

When Jesus calls us His friends in John 15:15, He isn't talking about a casual, surface-level friendship. He's talking about a deep, covenantal relationship, one rooted in trust, vulnerability, and intimacy. Like the disciples, we aren't just His followers. We aren't just His students. We are *His friends.* And because of that, He shares everything with us—His heart, His purpose, His plans.

But here's the thing: Friendship requires presence. It requires us to slow down long enough to experience it.

For years, I carried grief alone, not because God wasn't present, but because I didn't acknowledge that He was the friend I had been longing for. I had been burned in friendships before, so I didn't trust anyone with that level of vulnerability. I had convinced myself that no one could handle the burden I was carrying.

Rest is about being in the presence of someone safe.

But Jesus could. And He did. He didn't flinch at my sorrow. He didn't rush me through my emotions. He didn't say, "Come back when you've pulled yourself together." He *stayed*.

And that's what sets Jesus apart. His friendship isn't just supportive—it's steadfast. He doesn't wait for your best days. He sits with you in the worst ones. And while He can carry your emotional burdens, He doesn't start by fixing. He starts by being with you.

That's where rest comes from—not just in releasing what's heavy but in choosing to remain with the One who's already near. Because rest isn't just about putting something down. It's about being in the presence of someone safe. It's about knowing you're fully seen, fully known, and still fully loved.

So, if you've been carrying emotional weight—grief, shame, sadness, weariness—know this: You don't have to process it alone. Jesus, your Friend, is already here. His nearness is not earned. His presence is not conditional. He's not waiting for you to prove your strength. He's calling you to be still in His.

And maybe that's the shift today: not striving to have Jesus carry the weight but choosing to stay close to the One who *already* has.

Let yourself *release.*

Let yourself *rest.*

Let yourself *remain.*

Not just for what He can do, but because of who He is: a faithful friend. Present. Patient. With you.

Reflection Questions

1. What emotions come up when you think about Jesus calling you His friend? Does it feel natural or difficult to accept? Why?

2. Have you ever had a moment when you realized God was present, even though you hadn't acknowledged Him before? What was that experience like?

3. Have you ever struggled to trust Jesus with your emotional burdens? What fears or past experiences make it hard to let Him in?

Day 18

You did not choose me, but I chose you.
I appointed you to go and produce fruit
and that your fruit should remain.
—John 15:16

When you have four young kids, chances are that at least one of them will need something in the middle of the night. Maybe they have a bad dream. Maybe it's a lost blanket. Maybe they just want to be near a parent. But whatever it is, I have a habit that I probably shouldn't admit: I pretend to be asleep just to see which parent my child chooses.

I know, I know. Not my finest parenting moment. But when I'm warm, cozy, and finally getting some much-needed rest, I'm hoping—just this once—my child chooses their father instead of me. Because let's be real: Being chosen isn't always fun. Sometimes being chosen means sacrifice. It means being pulled from comfort, getting up when we'd rather stay put, showing up when we feel we have nothing left to give.

But not all choosing is like that. Some choosing is a gift. And that's what Jesus is saying in today's verse.

He chose us. Not out of obligation. Not because we were the only one available. Not with reluctance or hesitation. He chose us with love, on purpose, before we ever had a chance to prove ourselves. And that changes everything.

You didn't choose Him; He chose you.

You didn't choose Him; He chose you.

Perhaps those words hold significant weight because you've spent so much of your life feeling overlooked—wondering if you are enough, if you will ever be picked, if someone will see you and decide you are worth choosing. Maybe you've felt that way in relationships, in your career, or even in your faith journey, as if you need to somehow prove your worth before God will fully accept you.

But before you ever thought about Him, He already had you in mind.

This isn't about striving to be good enough or trying to earn His approval. This isn't about working your way up to Him. It's about His coming down to you, choosing you, and inviting you into a relationship where you can truly rest. First Peter 2:9 says, "But you are a

chosen race, a royal priesthood, a holy nation, a people for his possession, so that you may proclaim the praises of the one who called
you out of darkness into his marvelous light."

God didn't just choose you—He delights in you. He calls you His
special possession. You are His. No amount of failure or insecurity
or self-doubt can undo what He has already declared about you.

And because He chose you, you can rest. You don't have to over-
extend yourself proving your worth. You don't have to hustle for
belonging. You don't have to spend your life trying to earn a seat at
the table. The One who created the table has already pulled out a
chair for you.

Jesus didn't just choose you; He appointed you. He didn't just
call you into a relationship with Him—He called you into His mission:
"You did not choose me, but I chose you and appointed you so that
you might go and bear fruit—fruit that will last" (John 15:16, NIV).

God's choosing is not just about identity; it's also about purpose.
He didn't pick you just so you could sit on the sidelines. He chose
you to live a life that produces fruit—not fruit that fades but fruit
that remains.

So what does that mean?

It's easy to read that and immediately think about accomplishments—
things we can do, goals we can achieve, ways we can prove that we are
bearing fruit. But Jesus is talking about something deeper than success. The fruit He calls us to is eternal. Galatians 5:22–23 reminds
us: "The fruit of the Spirit is love, joy, peace, patience, kindness,
goodness, faithfulness, gentleness, and self-control." We can't measure these things in numbers or trophies. They're the qualities that

shape our lives, influence others, and ultimately bring glory to God.

And the best part? You're not responsible for producing the fruit. Jesus is the vine. The Father is the gardener. Your job is to remain. When you stay connected to Him, the fruit will naturally grow.

This is where rest comes in.

Because when you believe you've been chosen . . .

When you understand that God has already appointed you . . .

When you trust that He is the One producing the fruit in you . . .

You don't have to carry the pressure of proving yourself.

You don't have to burn yourself out trying to manufacture results.

You don't have to live with the anxiety of wondering whether you're doing enough.

Instead, you can rest in Him, trusting that who He is matters more than what we do.

When we try to carry everything ourselves, when we exhaust ourselves trying to prove our worth, when we forget that we are already chosen, we step outside the rest that Jesus is offering us.

But He is always inviting us back. To step away from the hustle. To stop trying to earn what has already been freely given. To breathe deep. To trust that because He chose us, He will sustain us.

As you go about your day, remember . . .

You are chosen.

You are appointed.

And you are sustained by the One who will never stop choosing you.

So, rest in Him. Trust Him. And let Him do the work.

Reflection Questions

1. What does it mean to you to be chosen by God? How does this truth shape the way you see yourself, especially in moments when you feel overlooked or unworthy?

2. In what ways can you remain in Jesus today, trusting Him to produce fruit through you instead of striving to do it on your own?

3. Think about the kind of fruit in your life that has the potential to remain. What gifts or opportunities can you use to reflect His love and make an eternal impact?

Day 19

Whatever you ask the Father
in my name, he will give you.
—John 15:16

Selling our home wasn't just a decision—it was a necessity.

We had exhausted every other option. The emergency fund was gone. We had dipped into our kids' savings, stretched every dollar, prayed every prayer, and still nothing. No financial cushion. No backup plan. Just bills stacking up and a mortgage we could no longer afford.

So, we did what we felt we had no other choice but to do: We put our house on the market.

At first, things looked promising. The house was staged, the pictures were taken, and we had an offer above asking immediately following the first showing. *This is it!* we thought. *God is making a way!*

But then the buyers backed out.

Another offer came, but they backed out too. Then another. And another. Each time, we would find ourselves back at square one, watching the weeks pass, our savings dwindle, and the uncertainty press harder against our chests.

I remember waking up one morning feeling the weight of it all. Isaiah 40:31 fell heavy on my heart:

> Those who wait on the LORD
> Shall renew their strength;
> They shall mount up with wings like eagles,
> They shall run and not be weary,
> They shall walk and not faint. (NKJV)

The words "they shall" stuck out to me. Other translations say "they will." It wasn't a maybe. It wasn't a possibility. It was a promise.

But before "they shall" comes "wait on the LORD." Trusting Him. Resting in Him—not just believing He *could* make a way but trusting that He *would*.

Up until that point, I had been carrying the burden of this situation on my own shoulders. I had prayed, yes, but I had also strategized, problem-solved, and exhausted every ounce of my mental energy trying to figure it out. I was attempting to control a situation that was completely out of my hands.

But that morning, something shifted. I realized there was nothing more I could do but wait. I had prayed. I had exhausted all my own resources. I had done everything within my ability to resolve the situation, to position the house for a buyer. But no amount of effort could force the outcome.

I let go.

I took God at His word, choosing to trust that He would do what only He could do. Because "those who wait on the LORD shall renew their strength." And at that point? I had no strength left. I had to rest in the arms of the Lord. I had to rest in who He is—Jehovah Jireh, my provider. The One who had never failed me before and wasn't about to start now.

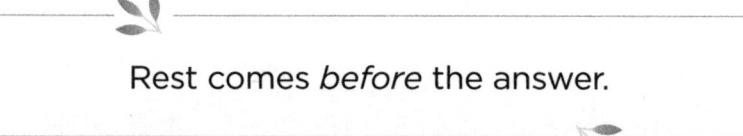

Rest comes *before* the answer.

And in the release, I found rest. In surrender, I found peace. Not because I had an answer in hand, but because I knew the One who held it.

When Jesus says, "Whatever you ask the Father in my name, he will give you," He's not giving us an open invitation to have everything we desire. He's welcoming us into something deeper: prayer that is rooted in trust, prayer that is surrendered to His will, prayer that is less about getting what we want and more about aligning our hearts with His.

Because rest comes *before* the answer. Because when you trust the One you're asking, you don't have to hold the outcome in your hands. You can let go. You can exhale. You can rest.

Jesus is inviting us in this verse to rest in the assurance that our prayers are heard. To release the burden of figuring it out and trust that He is already working on our behalf.

Today, ask boldly. Trust fully. And rest—not because you know *how* He will answer, but because you know *He will.*

And that's enough.

Reflection Questions

1. Think about a time when you prayed for something specific but had to wait for an answer. How did that season of waiting shape your trust in God?

2. When you pray, are you more focused on the outcome you desire or on aligning your heart with God's will? What helps you stay anchored in Him while you wait?

3. Resting in God's provision means releasing control. What is something you need to release today so that you can fully trust Him to provide in His perfect timing?

Day 20

This is what I command you:
Love one another.
—John 15:17

There was a time my two oldest boys got into it over something, though I can't remember what it was. Maybe it was a toy, maybe one of them said something that set the other off, maybe it was just one of those days when everything turns into a fight. Whatever it was, it had escalated enough that my husband and I knew we needed to step in.

But instead of just handing down a punishment and moving on, we wanted to take the opportunity to teach them something—something that we hoped would stick with them long after childhood. We wanted them to truly understand what it means not just to love each other but to love each other well.

So we thought about it. We weighed our options. And then we landed on something that, at the time, probably felt like the worst consequence ever: They had to work together to complete a five-hundred-piece puzzle before they could have any screen time.

This may not seem like a challenge, but for their age at the time, it was appropriate. Trust me. This was not a one-hour, easy, knock-it-out kind of thing. This was going to take time, patience, and teamwork—things they were not demonstrating in that moment.

Before we even handed them the puzzle, we sat them down and had a conversation. We talked about their actions, about how they had treated each other, about how their words and behavior did not reflect the kind of love we expected them to show as brothers. We reminded them that, no matter what, they are family. And family looks out for each other. Family speaks with kindness. Family loves—even when it's hard, even when you don't feel like it, even when you're frustrated with the person sitting across from you.

And then we gave them the puzzle.

As we eavesdropped, we noticed they had come up with a strategy. Instead of working against each other, they decided to divide and conquer—each brother taking on a different section of the puzzle. At first, the tension in the room was thick. They worked in silence, neither one wanting to ask the other for help.

But as time passed, something shifted. The frustration began to fade, and the room filled with quiet conversation. A joke here. A laugh there. Before long, they were back to enjoying each other's company the way they usually did.

Then, something unexpected happened. One of them finished his section first. He could have easily walked away, declared himself done, and left his brother to struggle through the rest alone. But instead of saying, "Well, I did my part—good luck with the rest," he simply kept going.

He stayed. He helped. He leaned in. By the time the final piece was set into place, they weren't just finished with the puzzle—they had built something together. The process that started with conflict ended with connection. In the end, they didn't just complete the task; they found joy in doing it together.

That night, we had another conversation with them. We talked about what they learned. We reinforced why we had given them this task in the first place. And, as we also do when we discipline our kids, we looked them in the eyes and said, "Now listen. If you didn't hear anything else, hear this." Then, we reminded them again, "This is how you love each other. You don't just tolerate one another. You don't just coexist. You show up, you serve, you help, you care. You love each other well."

And in John 15:17, that's exactly what Jesus is commanding us to do.

Jesus has spent this entire conversation pouring into His disciples, telling them about love, about remaining, about joy, about laying down their lives for one another. And then, before wrapping it up, He gives one final command: "Love one another."

It's like He's saying, "If you don't remember anything else, remember this: Love each other."

This isn't just another command—it's the period at the end of a beautiful, life-changing sentence.

Think about what Jesus has been saying up until this point:

As the Father has loved me, I have also loved you. Remain in my love. (John 15:9)

This is my command: Love one another as I have loved you. (verse 12)

No one has greater love than this: to lay down his life for his friends. (verse 13)

Over and over, He has been laying the foundation: Love is not optional. It is the defining mark of those who remain in Him. It's the evidence that we truly belong to Him. It's what binds us together as His people.

And now He reinforces it one last time. It's as if He's saying, "After everything I've told you, here's what I need you to hold on to. Here's what I need you to live out. Love each other."

Why does He repeat it? Because He knows how easy it is to forget. He knows how quickly we slip into selfishness, division, comparison, and bitterness. He knows that loving others—truly loving them—will require more than just a warm feeling. It will require intentionality, sacrifice, and a continual reliance on Him.

But what does love have to do with rest?

Everything.

Because true rest isn't just about stepping away from work or paring back our schedules. It's about stepping into the kind of life Jesus invites us into—one in which we are deeply connected to Him and deeply connected to one another.

When we carry bitterness, unforgiveness, or resentment, we are restless. Our souls stay in a state of turmoil, weighed down by unspoken words, unresolved conflicts, and unmet expectations. But when we choose to love—when we release offense, when we extend grace, when we forgive even when it's hard—we find rest.

Love is what keeps us connected, both to Him and to one another.

Love is an exhale. Love is a release. Love is where the pressure fades and grace takes its rightful place. This is why Jesus ends this passage in Scripture with this command. Because love is the rhythm that sustains us. Love is what keeps us connected, both to Him and to one another.

As we prepare to move into the last section of this devotional (*Remain*), this is the invitation: Don't just experience His love—stay in it. Don't just receive His love—reflect it.

This is what He commands. This is what we carry forward.

Love one another. And in doing so, we find rest.

Reflection Questions

1. Think about a time when choosing to love someone—despite frustration, conflict, or hurt—brought unexpected connection or healing. What did that experience teach you about the power of love?

2. Jesus repeats His command to love one another, emphasizing its importance. In what areas of your life do you find it hardest to live this out? What might it look like to lean into His love to make it possible?

3. How does love bring rest? Are there any grudges, burdens, or tensions in your heart that are keeping you restless? What would it look like to release those things and embrace the rhythm of love that Jesus invites us into?

Remain

Day 21

My husband pulled up to the airport curb and put the car in Park. The hum of rolling suitcases, the shuffle of feet, the occasional car horn—it all faded into the background. This moment felt too heavy to be drowned out by the ordinary.

We sat there for a second, neither of us quite ready to move.

Then, he turned to me. "I love you."

We hugged, but it wasn't one of those long, lingering embraces that melted away tension. No, this hug was hesitant, filled with unspoken emotions. A quiet understanding passed between us.

I need to go.

I know.

I don't want to leave you in this grief.

I don't want you to go, but I know you need this.

I didn't watch him drive away. I just turned, wiped silent tears from my face, and walked into the airport, carrying the guilt of my decision like an overstuffed carry-on. I felt guilty for leaving my husband in the fresh sting of grief after losing his sister. Guilty for stepping away from my family for three whole weeks. Guilty for the inevitable judgment from others who might not understand why I needed to do this.

But beneath the guilt was something else: hope. A small but steady assurance that I was walking toward something deeply necessary. A chance to heal, to rest, to let God do the kind of work that couldn't happen in the noise of my everyday life.

I was headed to a therapy intensive on Fox Island—a place where I would spend three weeks in silence and solitude, peeling back layers of grief, pain, and self-protection I hadn't realized I had built up over the years.

And before I could arrive, before I could even begin, I had to release.

Release the guilt.

Release the shame.

Release the weight of what people might think.

Release my need to be everything for everyone.

Only then could I walk fully into what God had for me.

The drive to Fox Island was beautiful. As I crossed the bridge, the waters stretched out on either side of me like something out of a painting. Trees, vibrant with reds and yellows of autumn, lined the winding roads. It was picturesque—calming, even. My shoulders, tense from weeks of carrying the burden of it all, finally began to relax.

But when I pulled up to the house where I would be staying, I couldn't help but feel underwhelmed. It was small and outdated. As I walked in, I noticed it smelled a little stale. Nothing about it felt like the kind of place where a life-changing encounter with God would happen.

But I wasn't there for an aesthetic experience. I was there for the work.

At first, I busied myself, putting away groceries, unpacking my bags, setting out my journal and Bible. But then came the moment when there was nothing left to do. Just me, the silence, and God.

I exhaled.

And then, over the next three weeks, I broke. I wept. I unraveled. I uncovered wounds I didn't even know I was carrying. I let the Lord into places I had unknowingly locked Him out of.

And through all of it, I was held.

The breaking didn't destroy me—it freed me. The undoing didn't leave me empty—it made room for healing. The silence wasn't lonely—it was filled with the presence of a God who had been there all along, waiting for me to slow down long enough to notice Him.

I had come to this place to remain with Him. But before I could, I had to release everything else. Before I could remain, I had to rest in the truth of who He is: Jehovah Jireh. My Provider.

Not just for me while I was here on this island but for my husband at home. For my kids in my absence. For the gaps I thought only I could fill.

And then, just as quickly as it all began, it was time to leave.

Coming home was a shock to my system. Three weeks in silence, stillness, and deep healing—and now I was stepping back into the noise, the responsibilities, the everyday rhythms of life that had not changed while I was away.

It was easy to experience God on Fox Island. There was space. There were no distractions. There were no dishes to wash or emails to answer or homeschool lessons to plan and teach. Just me and Him.

But remaining in Him? Remaining when the world around me was moving at full speed again? That was the real challenge.

And that's the challenge for all of us, isn't it? It's easy to seek God when life slows down, when we have those mountaintop moments where He feels close and tangible. But remaining isn't about the mountaintop. It's about choosing to stay connected to Him when life feels ordinary, when things feel messy, when our hearts feel distant.

Jesus doesn't just meet us in the silence. He meets us in the chaos too.

Jesus knew this when He spoke to His disciples in John 15. He had just spent time pouring into them, preparing them for what was to come. He had washed their feet, shared a meal, spoken of love and abiding. And now, as they walked toward the garden where He would be arrested, He gave them something to hold on to.

Because the mountaintop moment was about to end. Things were about to get dark. And when the world would tell them to scatter, to retreat, to lose hope, Jesus was calling them to remain.

"Remain in me, and I in you" (John 15:4).

Not just when it's easy.

Not just when it's quiet.

Not just when life slows down enough to make space.

Remain always.

Because the beauty of abiding in Jesus isn't just about the moments we feel His presence. It's also about knowing that even when we don't feel it, even when we feel like we've lost the closeness, He has never let us go.

I didn't stay on Fox Island. I went home. Then I had to make the intentional choice, every day, to remain. And that's what this final section of the devotional will explore—what it means to remain when life isn't still, when the mountaintop experience is behind us, when we feel distant or distracted or discouraged.

Jesus doesn't just meet us in the silence. He meets us in the chaos too. And He's inviting us not just to seek Him in the moments when it feels easy but to remain in Him always.

Hated but Held

THE INVITATION TO REMAIN

Read these words from the final part of John 15. Imagine yourself, once again, on a walk with Jesus. You're hanging on every word from your friend and teacher. Allow yourself to be surprised and confused as you listen to the final part of this chapter. Read it out loud if that helps you enter more fully into the scene.

> If the world hates you, understand that it hated me before it hated you. If you were of the world, the world would love you as its own. However, because you are not of the world, but I have chosen you out of it, the world hates you. Remember the word I spoke to you: "A servant is not greater than his master." If they persecuted me, they will also persecute you. If they kept my word, they will also keep yours. But they will do all these things to you on account of my name, because they don't know the one who sent me. If I had not come and spoken to them, they would not be guilty of sin. Now they have no excuse for their sin. The one who hates me also hates my Father. If I had not done the works among them that no one else has done, they would not be guilty of sin. Now they have seen and hated both me and my Father. But this happened so that the statement written in their law might be fulfilled: They hated me for no reason.
>
> When the Counselor comes, the one I will send to you from the Father—the Spirit of truth who proceeds from the Father—he will testify about me. You also will testify, because you have been with me from the beginning. (verses 18–27)

Journal

After your own mountaintop experiences with God, how do you typically respond when life returns to normal? Do you lean into Him, or do you find yourself drifting? How can you remind yourself daily that He is near, even when life feels chaotic? Use the space below to journal your answers.

_____

_____

_____

_____

_____

_____

_____

_____

_____

_____

_____

_____

Day 22

There are some conversations you never want to have with your children.

This was one of them.

It was 2020, and the world was heavy. There had been yet another public murder of a Black man at the hands of a police officer, and the air was thick with pain, grief, and tension. My husband and I knew that we couldn't shield our boys from the reality of the world they were growing up in. They were getting older, more independent. They were spending more time outside of our care, and we couldn't always be there to protect them.

So, we sat them down. And with love and honesty, we told them the truth: "There are people in this world who will look at you and make assumptions about who you are. Not because they know you. Not because of how you treat people. But because of the color of your skin."

We didn't say it to scare them. We said it to prepare them.

We talked through how to interact with authority figures. What to do if they were ever stopped by police. How to make sure they came home safe.

Then we looked them in the eyes and said something just as important: "You are a Black boy growing into a Black man in America. And yes, there are people who will make unfair judgments about you. But that does not change who you are. And it does not change how you love." We told them, "You will love God, you will love yourself, and you will love people. Period."

It was a hard conversation. One that no parent should have to have. But it was necessary.

Recently, as I read Jesus's words in John 15, I realized this is exactly what He was doing for His disciples. In the previous verses, Jesus spoke about love, telling them to remain in His love and to love one another. But now He makes a sharp turn: "If the world hates you, keep in mind that it hated Me first."

Wait—what?

After all this talk about love, now He's talking about hate?

Yes. Because just like my husband and I had to prepare our boys for the reality of the world they are growing up in, Jesus was preparing His disciples for the reality they were about to step into.

They had walked with Him, watched Him love people with kindness and compassion, and seen Him bring healing and hope. But now Jesus was saying, "The world isn't going to celebrate you for following Me. In fact, it's going to hate you for it." Jesus knew how deeply the world would reject them. He knew they would be ridiculed, arrested, beaten, and even killed for the sake of His name. And just like any good parent, He wasn't going to send them into that without warning them first.

Jesus said, "If you were of the world, the world would love you as its own. However, . . . you are not of the world . . . I have chosen you out of it." This is the tension we live in as followers of Jesus. We don't belong to the world anymore. We are set apart. And that means there will be conflict between what we believe and what the world expects from us.

He didn't let hatred change how He loved—
He loved even unto death.

There will be moments when standing firm in Christ costs you something. When loving Jesus means losing the approval of others. When choosing integrity, righteousness, or faithfulness makes you an outsider.

Maybe you've felt this tension before. Maybe you've lost friendships because of your faith. Maybe you've had to walk away from certain opportunities because they didn't align with what you knew was right. Maybe you've felt the sting of being misunderstood, rejected, or even ridiculed for choosing to follow Jesus.

The world may hate you, but you are called to remain. To remain in love. To remain in integrity. To remain in truth. To remain because Jesus remained. He didn't run from rejection—He endured it. He didn't bow to pressure—He stood firm. He didn't let hatred change how He loved—He loved even unto death.

I think about my boys. How, one day, they'll step out into the world without me by their side. How they'll be faced with choices, challenges, and moments when doing the right thing will cost them something. And I pray that when those moments come, they will remain.

I pray they'll remember the love of their parents, the truth of who they are, and the faith that grounds them. I pray they'll choose to love even when the world doesn't love them back. I pray they'll stand firm in Christ, no matter what comes.

Because this is what it means to be chosen by Him.

And if we remain, we can trust that He will always remain with us too. Jesus's words in John 15:18–19 are not just a warning—they're a call to faithfulness.

The world will never fully understand the way of Jesus. It will always push back against His love, His truth, His righteousness. But we are not of this world. We have been chosen out of it. And that means that no matter what comes, we remain.

Even when it's hard.

Even when it costs us something.

Even when the world hates us.

Because the love of Jesus is worth more than anything the world could ever offer.

And that is why we remain.

Reflection Questions

1. Have you ever felt tension between remaining faithful to Jesus and fitting in? What was that experience like, and how did you respond?

2. In what areas of your life do you currently feel pressure to conform, and how might God be calling you to stand firm instead?

3. Remaining in Jesus requires trusting that He is enough, even when following Him comes with challenges. What fears or hesitations do you need to release in order to fully remain in Him?

Day 23

Remember the word I spoke to you:
"A servant is not greater than his master."
If they persecuted me, they will also
persecute you. If they kept my word,
they will also keep yours.
—John 15:20

Okay, pop quiz time. Don't worry, I'm not grading you.

Jesus quotes Himself in this verse: "A servant is not greater than his master." Here's your question: When did He first say this to the disciples?

Was it when one of them, like Peter or Andrew, first decided to follow Him? Was it after a miracle, like raising Lazarus from the dead? Was it in response to a hard question from one of the religious leaders trying to trap Him?

Good guesses. But the first time Jesus said these words was actually earlier that same evening.

Let me set the scene.

Before the disciples took this nighttime walk with Jesus in John 15, they had dinner together—what we now call the Last Supper. And in the middle of this sacred meal, Jesus did something shocking. He stood up from the table, took off His outer robe, wrapped a towel around His waist, and picked up a bowl of water. Then He knelt to wash His disciples' feet.

Then, after washing all their feet, He looked them in the eye and said, "I have given you an example, that you also should do just as I have done for you. Truly I tell you, a servant is not greater than his master, and a messenger is not greater than the one who sent him" (John 13:15–16).

Now, a short while later, Jesus is repeating those words: "A servant is not greater than his master." But this time, He's not talking about washing feet. He's talking about persecution. It's as if He's saying, "Just as I served, you must serve. Just as I suffered, you must be willing to suffer."

Jesus is telling us that remaining in Him comes with a cost. If He was rejected, we will be too. If He was misunderstood, we will be too. If He was hated by the world, we shouldn't be surprised when the world hates us too.

And listen, I don't know about you, but I don't love that.

I like being liked. I like knowing that people understand me, respect me, and receive what I have to say with open hearts. I want to serve others and have that service be appreciated. But Jesus is telling us plainly that that won't always happen.

This is where faith stops being comfortable: when following Jesus means risking misunderstanding or rejection, even from people we deeply care about. This is where following Jesus stops being easy, where the cost starts feeling too high, where the call to remain starts feeling too weighty.

Because when you're doing everything *right*—when you're loving people well, serving faithfully, speaking truth in love—and you still get rejected? That's when the temptation to water down your faith, to blend in, to shrink back, starts to feel strong. That's when doubt creeps in.

Why am I doing this if it only makes things harder? Is staying faithful really worth the cost?

Jesus knew we'd ask those questions. And that's why He didn't sugarcoat it. He didn't want His disciples—or us—to be blindsided when obedience led to opposition.

He's letting us know that living for Him will come with moments of rejection. And not just from strangers but also from people close to us, from those we care about. Jesus Himself was betrayed by a close friend, abandoned by His followers, and rejected by His own people. If it happened to Him, we can expect it will happen to us too.

But here's the hope: We are never alone in it.

Jesus isn't asking us to experience anything He hasn't already endured Himself. He was slandered, mocked, and abandoned by people He loved. He served people who never thanked Him. He gave His life for people who spit in His face. And yet, He remained faithful and is asking us to do the same.

So, when you remain in Him, you're not just standing firm in your beliefs but you're standing with the One who understands your pain, who strengthens you when you're weary, who holds you fast when you feel like giving up.

You're standing with the One who understands your pain, who strengthens you when you're weary, who holds you fast when you feel like giving up.

And listen, remaining doesn't mean winning. It doesn't mean every seed you plant will grow. It doesn't mean every act of love will be reciprocated. It doesn't mean you'll always see the fruit of your faithfulness.

Remaining means staying planted even when nothing seems to be happening. Remaining means trusting that, even when rejection stings, you are still exactly where you're supposed to be. Remaining means refusing to let hardship be the reason you stop.

So if you've ever been misunderstood, overlooked, or mistreated for trying to follow Jesus, take heart. You're in good company. And the One you're remaining in? He's worth it.

Reflection Questions

1. Think of a time when you have felt discouraged because your faith was met with rejection or resistance. How does knowing that Jesus experienced the same thing encourage you to remain in Him?

2. In what areas of your life are you tempted to give up or shrink back when following Jesus feels hard?

3. The next time you face opposition because of your faith, how can you lean into the promise that when you remain in Jesus, you are never alone?

Day 24

Have you ever been completely misunderstood?

I mean the kind of misunderstanding that leaves you frustrated because no matter how much you try to explain yourself, the other person just *does not get it*. Maybe they assumed something about you that wasn't true. Maybe they judged your motives unfairly. Maybe they reacted to you based on their own past experiences rather than who you actually are.

It's frustrating, isn't it? It makes you want to defend yourself, set the record straight, and prove your heart was in the right place.

Now, imagine being *Jesus*.

Jesus, the One who came to *save* the world, was completely misunderstood by it. He came in love, yet He was hated. He healed the sick, yet He was rejected. He spoke truth, yet He was accused of blasphemy.

Why?

Because *they didn't know what they didn't know.*

I've learned this lesson the hard way as a parent. There have been plenty of times when I've been *absolutely sure* I knew exactly what happened between my kids, only to find out later that I had it all wrong.

You know the scene: One kid comes running, tears streaming, breathless with frustration. "He hit me!" "She took my toy!" "They won't share!" And before I even get a full grasp of the situation, I'm already looking at the other child—the one standing there with a guilty expression, bracing for impact. My mom brain is making calculations at lightning speed: *This one looks innocent. That one looks guilty. Case closed.*

Except . . . then comes the rest of the story.

"No, Mom, you don't understand. He didn't mean to hit me. He was reaching for his book and bumped into me."

"Wait, Mom, she didn't just take my toy. I told her she could have a turn, and then I changed my mind."

"Mom, I wasn't ignoring you. I genuinely didn't hear you."

And just like that, I realize I got it wrong. I made an assumption. I thought I knew. But I didn't know what I didn't know.

And Jesus is saying, "That's exactly what's happening in the world." In this passage, Jesus is explaining why His followers will face rejection: "They will treat you this way because of my name, for they do not know the one who sent me" (NIV).

They don't know. They think they do, but they don't. The religious leaders of Jesus's time thought they knew God, but they didn't recognize Him when He was standing right in front of them. The crowds thought they knew what kind of Messiah they wanted, but they rejected the One who actually came to save them.

And even today, people resist Christ, dismiss His followers, or even outright reject the gospel. Why? Because they don't know Him.

They don't know the heart of Jesus—the One who welcomed sinners, healed the broken, and laid down His life for people who didn't even ask Him to. They don't know the Father who sent Him—the God of mercy, justice, and love. They don't know the freedom He offers, the grace He gives, or the rest that comes from knowing you are fully loved.

They think they do, but they don't. And because of that, they'll misunderstand us too. Our job is not to fight for our own defense or to get caught up in shock and offense. It's to remain in Christ, love, and the truth that Jesus prepared us for.

So, what do we do when we're misunderstood? When people assume things about our faith, our choices, our convictions? When standing for truth costs us friendships, invitations, or opportunities?

We remain.

We remain in the truth that Jesus went through this first. He was misunderstood, misrepresented, and mistreated. Yet, He never stopped loving. He never stopped reaching out. He never stopped offering grace.

We remain in the truth that we don't have to take it personally.

Jesus said it plainly: "They will treat you this way because of my name" (NIV). It's not really about you. It's about their own lack of understanding.

We remain in the truth that only the Holy Spirit can open eyes. No amount of arguing, debating, or proving ourselves will do what only God can do. He is the One who reveals truth. Our job is to remain faithful.

We remain in the truth that love is always the better response. When we face opposition, we don't react with defensiveness or bitterness. Instead, we respond with the same love Jesus showed—even to those who nailed Him to a cross.

Remain in the truth that love is always the better response.

So, the next time you feel rejected, misunderstood, or dismissed because of your faith, take a deep breath. Remember: They don't know what they don't know.

And then ask yourself: How can I remain in Christ today? How can I respond like Jesus? How can I trust that God is at work—even when I can't see it?

Because you *do* know. You know the One who sent Jesus. You know the One who called you by name. You know the One who is worth remaining in.

So, *remain.*

Reflection Questions

1. Describe a time when you realized you didn't know what you didn't know. How did the moment of revelation shift your perspective, and what did you learn from it?

2. When have you felt misunderstood or rejected because of your faith? How did you respond?

3. In what ways can you respond with love instead of defensiveness when others don't understand your faith?

Day 25

If I had not come and spoken to them,
they would not be guilty of sin.
Now they have no excuse for their sin.
—John 15:22

et me tell you a little something about my family and the dishwasher. As a recovering perfectionist and people pleaser, I'll admit that loading the dishwasher has been a source of disproportionate frustration in my household. I used to expect everyone in my family—husband, kids, whoever was helping—to just *know* how to load it properly. In my mind, it was simple, self-explanatory, even. Plates in the bottom rack, bowls angled correctly, cups facing downward to avoid the dreaded water pool. Yet time and again, I'd open the dishwasher to find chaos: cups upright, bowls sideways, plates stacked like a game of *Tetris* gone wrong.

I'd get frustrated. *Why don't they just know how to do this?* I'd think. But the truth was, I hadn't taught them. I had assumed they'd figure it out. Once I realized that my frustration stemmed from unmet expectations, I decided to take a different approach. I started showing them how to load the dishes. And I didn't just show them once—I model it repeatedly. We revisit it often (and prayerfully, one day, they'll get it!).

Here's the thing: I realized that their lack of understanding wasn't intentional. They weren't trying to annoy me—they just didn't know better. Once I taught them, however, they couldn't use the excuse of ignorance anymore.

Now, I know this is a lighthearted example, but it's a perfect way to approach what Jesus is saying in this verse. He's addressing a fundamental truth: When people are confronted with the reality of who He is and the truth He brings, they can no longer claim ignorance.

Before Jesus came, humanity had only a limited understanding of God's standards. But Jesus made them clear through His words, His miracles, and His sacrifice. He didn't just speak truth; He is truth. In John 14:6, He declared, "I am the way, the truth, and the life. No one comes to the Father except through me." Jesus wasn't offering just another perspective—He was revealing the only path to God, the only way to life.

And when truth like that is revealed, it demands a response.

By exposing the depth of sin and the reality of salvation, Jesus left people without excuse. His words and actions made it impossible to stay neutral. Some responded with faith, surrender, and transformation. Others resisted, rejected, and even hated Him for it.

And the same is true for us today.

When we remain in Christ, we carry His truth with us. That

means we will have moments where we bring truth into someone's life—whether through our words, actions, or simply the way we live. And just like with my dishwasher situation, when people are shown the truth, they can no longer claim they don't know.

But here's the challenge: People don't always receive the truth with open arms.

Have you ever had a moment when you knew better but didn't want to do better? Maybe it was a conviction from the Holy Spirit, a difficult truth spoken by a friend, or a lesson you had to learn the hard way. The truth has a way of exposing what's really in our hearts—and sometimes, it's uncomfortable.

We don't change hearts; Jesus does.

That's why our role isn't just to point people to truth and walk away. Our calling is to remain: to stay present, to walk alongside others with patience and grace, just as Jesus has done for us.

This is a process, not a onetime event. It's the continual work of revealing Christ's love, offering grace, and standing firm in truth, even when it's uncomfortable. It's showing up, over and over, modeling what it means to follow Jesus.

As we do, we can rest in knowing that the outcome isn't on us. We don't change hearts; Jesus does. Our job is to remain faithful, to keep loving, and to keep pointing to the One who has already revealed Himself to us.

So, don't be discouraged if someone doesn't immediately receive the truth. Don't let rejection keep you from loving well. Keep showing up. Keep remaining in Him. Because the more you remain, the more you reflect His light. And the more His light shines, the more others will see the truth for themselves.

Reflection Questions

1. Have you ever experienced a moment when Jesus revealed a truth to you that was hard to accept? How did you respond, and what did you learn through that process?

2. Jesus said, "I am the way, the truth, and the life" (John 14:6). In what ways does remaining in Him help you walk in truth, even when it's uncomfortable or challenging?

3. Think of someone in your life who has yet to embrace the truth of Jesus. How can you remain present with love and grace, modeling His truth without pressuring them to change?

Day 26

The one who hates me also hates my Father.
If I had not done the works among them
that no one else has done, they would not be
guilty of sin. Now they have seen and
hated both me and my Father.

—John 15:23–24

Have you ever had a conversation about faith that left you feeling defeated?

Some time ago, I was talking with someone I love and respect—someone who had seen God's hand on my life in undeniable ways. They'd witnessed the ways He'd provided, how He'd led me through hard seasons, how my life has been shaped and softened by His presence. But when I brought up Jesus, I could sense the tension rise. They weren't open. In fact, the more we talked, the more closed off they became. And I left that conversation with a heavy heart.

How could they see so much of God's goodness and still not believe? How could they witness transformation and still walk away unchanged?

If you've ever experienced something like that—if you've poured out your heart and still felt shut down—you know how much it stings. Especially when it's someone close to you. Someone you've prayed for. Someone you want so desperately to know the Jesus who's changed everything for you.

And if that's you, I just want to say: You're not alone. Jesus prepared us for this.

In John 15, He's honest about what's ahead, not just for His disciples but also for us. People rejected Him, even after watching Him heal the blind, calm storms, feed thousands, and raise the dead. He said plainly, "They have seen and hated both me and my Father."

It's wild, isn't it? That people could see with their own eyes the works of God and still turn away? But Jesus knew what we sometimes forget: Seeing isn't the same as believing. Belief requires surrender. And surrender isn't easy. It's not just accepting that something is true—it's letting go of our control, our pride, and our desire to live life on our own terms. Belief means handing over the pen and letting Jesus write our story. It means trusting His authority, His timing, and His ways, even when they don't make sense. And for many, that's the hardest part—not the believing in miracles but the surrendering to the One who performs them.

Jesus wasn't rejected because people didn't fail to understand Him. He was rejected because they did. His works revealed the

truth—Jesus was the Son of God—and that truth demanded a response. Accepting who Jesus was meant reevaluating everything
they believed about God and about themselves. And some just
weren't ready to do that.

This is why *remaining* matters.

Remaining isn't just staying put when faith is easy. It's choosing
to keep showing up even when your prayers feel unanswered. It's
deciding to trust God's timing when the people you love still haven't
said yes to Him. It's sitting in the tension of hope and heartache—
and still holding on.

When I think about those conversations I've had—especially the
ones that felt like dead ends—I'm always grateful when someone
stays open, even a little. That willingness to talk gives me hope. And
after those moments, I usually take it all to the Lord in prayer. I ask
Him to water any seeds that may have been planted. To soften what
feels hard. To do the work I can't do. And yes, I get discouraged
sometimes. But at the end of the day, I know it's God who stirs
hearts. Not me.

And if I'm honest, I often find myself grieving for those who resist
Him. Because I know what they're missing. I know the peace He offers. The love that doesn't walk away. The grace that carries you
when nothing else can. And it hurts to watch people turn away from
that.

But even in the hurt, I'm learning to remain. To remain in prayer,
believing He's still working. To remain in love, even when conversations get hard. To remain in hope, knowing His timing is perfect. To
remain in truth, even when the rejection stings.

Because Jesus's identity hasn't changed. And neither has mine.

That's part of what rattled the religious leaders most—Jesus knew exactly who He was. His unity with the Father wasn't merely a theological claim; it was a declaration of identity. And when your identity is secure, it changes how you move through the world. Jesus didn't flinch. He didn't back down. He stood in truth, even when it cost Him everything.

Remain in the promise that He is still God.

And, friend, when you remain in Him, that identity—secure, chosen, and rooted in the love of the Father—becomes yours too. You don't have to hustle for validation. You don't have to earn God's attention. You are His. Fully known. Fully loved. Fully secure. So when others push back, misunderstand, or reject the Jesus you reflect, remember who you are. You are rooted in Him. Steady. Seen. Safe.

And if you're in that place today—if you've been showing up, praying, sharing, and still haven't seen the breakthrough—I want to encourage you: Remain in who He is. Remain in what you know. Remain in the promise that He is still God, even when people can't see it yet.

Take time to pray for the people in your life who are far from Him. Reflect on how He's transformed your life. And remind yourself that your job is faithfulness. You don't need to have all the answers. You don't need to fix anyone. You just need to remain. The rest is in His hands.

Reflection Questions

1. How does knowing Jesus was rejected—even after revealing the Father—encourage you to keep sharing your faith today?

2. Jesus says that the world saw His works and still hated Him. Why do you think some people reject Jesus, even when they witness His goodness? How does this truth challenge or encourage you in your own faith?

3. Think of someone in your life who has seen God's work but has not yet believed. How can you remain in Christ as you pray for them and continue to reflect His love?

Day 27

This happened so that the statement
written in their law might be fulfilled:
They hated me for no reason.
—John 15:25

I t was Christmas Eve. My family and I had just returned home
from an evening of caroling, our voices still warm from singing,
our hands wrapped around mugs of steaming beverages. The
house was buzzing with conversations and laughter, the scent of
fresh baked goodies lingering in the air. Joy filled the space as we
gathered together, unwinding from the night.

I wasn't expecting him.

My now-husband was supposed to be in Maryland visiting family
for the holidays, thousands of miles away from our little gathering.
But suddenly, I heard a familiar voice—his voice—coming down the
hallway, carrying words in rhythm and cadence. He was reciting the
same spoken word poem I'd heard years before, his footsteps steady

as he made his way toward me. The room fell silent as we turned to watch him, the air thick with anticipation.

My heart raced. What was happening? Was this real?

And then, as he reached me, he dropped to one knee.

I barely had time to process it before I heard myself whisper, "Of course!"

We stood in a circle that night, hands wrapped around plastic flutes of sparkling cider, hearts full, as our loved ones took turns speaking blessings over our engagement. It was a sacred, beautiful evening—one that would stay with me for years to come. But of all the words spoken that night, my mother's are the ones that I can still hear so clearly: "It's so obvious that God has His hand all over your union. Your marriage is going to bring Him glory. He's going to use it to bless others."

At the time, I felt the heaviness of her words, but I don't think I fully grasped them. I was in love. I was excited. I was ready to step into this new season with joy and confidence. What I didn't yet understand was how deeply I would have to hold on to God's presence in the years to come.

But you know what? My mom was right. Fifteen years later, I can say with confidence that our marriage has been a blessing—not just to us but also to the people we've had the honor of walking alongside, encouraging, and doing life with. But that doesn't mean it's been easy.

There have been seasons where marriage felt impossibly hard. Seasons where I wanted to throw in the towel and walk away because it felt like no matter how much we loved each other, no matter how much we respected each other, it was still hard. And I've had moments when I wondered, *If God's hand is really on this, why does it have to be so difficult?*

I imagine the disciples were asking a similar question. They had left everything to follow Jesus. They had seen Him perform miracles, heal the sick, and speak truth with authority. They knew He was the Messiah. And yet, what did they get in return? Opposition. Rejection. Hatred.

Jesus knew they were going to struggle with this, so He prepared them. He said, "This happened so that the statement written in their law might be fulfilled: They hated me for no reason."

He was connecting the dots for them, showing them that this opposition wasn't random; instead, it was part of God's bigger story.

The same is true for us.

Just like my mom's words over our marriage didn't mean we'd never struggle, Jesus's calling over the disciples didn't mean their path would be easy. In fact, it meant quite the opposite, which meant they were right where they were supposed to be.

And that's what remaining is all about.

Remaining isn't just about staying when it's easy. It's about staying when everything in you wants to leave. It's about holding on when faithfulness feels costly. When obedience leads to discomfort instead of ease. When your circumstances make you wonder, *God, is this really what You had in mind?*

Jesus was giving His disciples an anchor—something to hold on to when things got tough. He was showing them that their suffering wasn't meaningless. That even in rejection, they were still in the center of God's plan.

The disciples followed Jesus, walked with Him, listened to Him. And because they remained, Jesus revealed to them the deeper meaning of everything they had been taught. He even said it Himself: "I have called you friends, because I have made known to you everything I have heard from my Father" (John 15:15). In other words, He didn't just invite them to follow Him—He invited them to know the heart behind the mission. And that kind of closeness? It only comes from staying.

When we remain in Jesus—when we stay with Him through the doubts, the struggles, and the seasons that feel unbearable—He gives us clarity. He helps us see that even when things don't make sense, even when it feels like the world is against us, we are still in the middle of God's story.

When we remain in Jesus— when we stay with Him through the doubts, the struggles, and the seasons that feel unbearable—He gives us clarity.

If you're in a season where remaining feels more like enduring, hold on. If you're in a season where obedience feels like it's bringing you more resistance than reward, hold on. If you've ever wondered why faithfulness sometimes feels so hard, hold on. Because even in the struggle, you are still in the hands of a faithful God.

You might not see it yet, but one day you'll look back and realize that you were exactly where you were meant to be.

Reflection Questions

1. Jesus reminded His disciples that following Him would come with opposition, yet He reassured them with the truth of Scripture. Read Psalm 27:13–14. What does this passage invite you to believe or do as you wait on the Lord?

2. Think of a time when God was clearly at work in your life. How did He reveal His hand in that situation?

3. How have past experiences with God's faithfulness strengthened your faith?

Day 28

When the Counselor comes,
the one I will send to you from the Father—
the Spirit of truth who proceeds from
the Father—he will testify about me.
—John 15:26

Have you ever been somewhere unfamiliar and totally lost? I'm talking about the kind of lost where your GPS is glitching, the street signs don't make sense, and every turn seems to take you farther from where you need to be. It's frustrating, disorienting, and a little overwhelming.

I remember a time when I was driving to a friend's house in an unfamiliar part of town. My GPS was giving me delayed directions, so I kept missing turns and having to reroute. The more I tried to figure it out on my own, the more lost I became. At one point, I pulled into a parking lot just to breathe and reset. I needed to stop, get my bearings, and let my GPS catch up before I ended up even farther from my destination.

That moment reminded me of what it's like to navigate life without the Holy Spirit—disoriented, unsure, and desperately needing guidance. And honestly, that's how we feel in so many moments of life, especially in times of loss.

When someone we love passes away, we often go to great lengths to hold on to their memory. Whether it's cherishing keepsakes like their favorite sweater, a handwritten note, or a well-worn Bible, we cling to whatever reminds us of them. Some of us frame photos; others plant trees or wear special jewelry in their honor. It's all an attempt to keep a piece of their presence with us, a connection to the essence of who they were.

Now imagine the disciples. They had walked with Jesus every single day for three years. They had seen miracles, shared meals, and sat at His feet as He taught. They were closer to Him than they were to anyone else. And now He was telling them He was leaving.

Jesus knew the grief they would experience. He knew the panic, the fear, and the longing they would feel when He was gone. And He knew that no keepsake or physical reminder would be enough to sustain them.

So, what did Jesus do?

He promised them something far greater than a keepsake. He promised them a person.

When the Counselor comes, the one I will send to you
from the Father—the Spirit of truth who proceeds from the
Father—he will testify about me. (John 15:26)

Jesus gave them the Holy Spirit, not as a memory but as a living presence—a guide, a teacher, and a source of strength for everything that was ahead.

Depending on your Bible translation, the Holy Spirit is referred to as Counselor, Comforter, Advocate, or Helper—each name revealing a different aspect of His role in our lives. But there's one title that remains consistent: the Spirit of truth.

We don't just receive truth—we carry it. We live it. We share it.

And in a world that constantly distorts truth, we need the Spirit of truth now more than ever. Every day, we're bombarded with conflicting messages—on social media, in the news, through culture—telling us who we should be, what we should believe, and where we should place our hope. Without the Spirit, it's easy to get lost in the noise.

But Jesus made a promise. The Holy Spirit won't just offer helpful advice. He will speak on behalf of the Father, revealing eternal truths that we can trust completely. He will bring clarity where there is confusion, peace where there is fear, and conviction where there is compromise. And the Spirit will testify about Him—not about fleeting opinions, not about human wisdom, but about Jesus.

The Spirit's first work is to testify to us, reminding us of who Jesus is and what He has done. But His work doesn't stop there. As we remain in Jesus, the Spirit equips us to testify to others. We don't just receive truth—we carry it. We live it. We share it.

This is why remaining in Jesus isn't something we do alone. It requires help. It requires surrender. It requires the Spirit of truth leading us, shaping us, and making us more like Christ.

Here's the thing about the Spirit of truth: He can't lead us if we're clinging to our own understanding.

> Trust in the LORD with all your heart,
> and do not rely on your own understanding;
> in all your ways know him,
> and he will make your paths straight. (Proverbs 3:5–6)

To remain in Jesus means we surrender our need for control. It means we stop trying to navigate life on our own terms and instead follow His leading, even when we don't see the full picture.

Jesus's promise to send the Holy Spirit wasn't just a comforting thought for His disciples—it was a gift of immeasurable value. The Spirit of truth is still guiding, comforting, and equipping us today.

So, the question is, Will we let Him lead?

Let's remain in Him, trusting His voice above all others and allowing Him to testify through us to a world in desperate need of truth.

Reflection Questions

1. In what areas of your life do you need to surrender your understanding and trust the Spirit of truth to guide you?

2. How has the Holy Spirit testified to Jesus in your life recently?

3. What steps can you take to invite the Spirit of truth to help you remain in Christ this week?

Day 29

You also will testify . . .

—John 15:27

When people ask my husband how he started his business, I can almost always predict how he's going to answer. The story, which he tells often, always includes this pivotal moment when I unknowingly sparked something in him. One night, as we were lying in bed, I asked, "What's your five-year plan?" His response was classic: "I don't know. Whatever God has for me."

Now, I can admit I didn't handle that response with the grace you might expect. Instead, I said, "I'm trusting you with my family and our future, and you don't have the next five years planned?" And then—this part is my husband's favorite detail—I rolled over and went to sleep, leaving him wide awake and thinking.

It's one of our family's most shared stories, not because it's dramatic but because it's deeply meaningful. That conversation was a turning point for him and, ultimately, for our family. And you know what? I never get tired of hearing him tell it.

When it comes to telling stories about Jesus, though, I'll admit I sometimes lean on my actions more than my words. It's not that I don't want to talk about Him—I absolutely do—but I often hope that His light shining through my life will speak louder than anything I could say. I don't want to force-feed Jesus to anyone. I think there's a part of me that fears coming across as someone who's beating people over the head with the Bible.

Maybe you feel the same way. You don't hesitate to share about what Jesus has done in your life, but you prefer it to come through in how you live rather than what you say. And honestly, there's wisdom in that. Our actions can and should reflect Jesus in powerful ways. But as I reflect on this verse, I feel this nudge—this call—not only to live a testimony but to speak one too.

We're living in times when boldness about who Jesus is and what He's done feels increasingly necessary. The world is full of voices pulling people in every direction, and some of those voices lead to lies, confusion, and hopelessness. If we aren't willing to share the truth about Jesus, who will?

Testifying doesn't have to mean preaching a sermon or having all the answers. It doesn't mean beating people over the head with Scripture. It means sharing the story of who Jesus is in your life with honesty, humility, and love.

When Jesus says, "You also will testify," He's inviting us to take part in something eternal. Testifying is about joining Him in His mission to bring light into a dark world. And we're not doing it alone—the Holy Spirit is with us every step of the way.

It's important to remember that everyone's testimony looks different. Some people are gifted with the ability to share the gospel boldly and openly in large crowds. Others testify in quieter, more intimate ways—through one-on-one conversations, through encouragement, through music, poetry, storytelling, or other creative expressions that speak to the truth of who Jesus is.

If you're hesitant to testify because you don't want to come across as pushy or overbearing, take heart. Your testimony doesn't have to be perfect or polished; it just has to be honest. Share what Jesus has done in your life. Share how He's carried you through difficult seasons, how He's provided for you, and how He's changed your heart. People are drawn to authenticity, not perfection.

Remember, when you testify about Jesus, the Spirit is right there, guiding your words and opening hearts. You don't have to rely on your own strength or ability. The Holy Spirit does the heavy lifting.

The Holy Spirit does the heavy lifting.

So start where you are. Share what Jesus has done in your life, even if it feels small or unfinished. You don't need the whole picture— just the piece you've lived. Because when you remain in Him, your life begins to speak. And that voice? That testimony? It matters.

When Jesus told His disciples, "You also will testify," it was not a command to perform. Instead, it was a promise of what would naturally flow from a life lived with Him. And while He didn't stop there, that's where we pause today—with the invitation to live in such a way that your life speaks.

Because when you remain close to Jesus, the story will come. And tomorrow, we'll look at why. Because there's power in proximity, and remaining changes everything.

Reflection Questions

1. What is a specific way Jesus has shown His love and faith-fulness in your life that you can share with someone today?

2. When have you hesitated to speak about Jesus, relying more on your actions? How might the Holy Spirit be nudging you to share your story with words?

3. Who in your life needs to hear your testimony about what Jesus has done for you? Write down what the Holy Spirit is inviting you to share with that person.

Day 30

Because you have been with me
from the beginning.

—John 15:27

There's something unique about people who've been with you from the beginning. The ones who have seen the full story—not just the highlight reel but the late nights, the ordinary Tuesdays, the difficult decisions, and the long in-between. That kind of closeness can't be manufactured. It's forged in time and presence. And as Jesus prepares His disciples for what's ahead, He tells them plainly: "You also will testify, because you have been with me from the beginning."

We've all worked with people, right? Eight hours a day, five days a week, for months or even years. And yet, even with all that time spent together, it's possible to still know next to nothing about them. Sure, you might exchange casual small talk, commiserate over deadlines, or share a few laughs in the break room—but the relationship often stops there. Just because you're near someone doesn't mean you really know them.

But the disciples weren't just co-workers with Jesus. They didn't simply show up for the miracles and then clock out. They remained. They followed Him from town to town. They shared meals, watched Him heal, listened to Him teach, and witnessed Him retreat to pray. They saw His joy, His exhaustion, His compassion. They asked questions, got it wrong, then asked again. They were close enough to see the humanity and the divinity—and that changed them.

Jesus wasn't giving them a job description when He told them they would testify. Instead, He was pointing to their lived experience. Their nearness to Him. The transformation that came simply from being with Him. Because they remained, their lives were marked by His presence. And that kind of transformation always speaks.

He's saying the same to us.

The reason you can testify is not because you've mastered Scripture or memorized the right answers. It's because you've been with Him. You've walked through seasons of joy and struggle, of celebration and grief. You've prayed desperate prayers and whispered thanks. You've seen Him provide, comfort, correct, and heal. You've remained.

And remaining changes you.

It bears fruit—not always immediately and not always in the ways you expect. But it's there. Love, joy, peace, patience, kindness, goodness, faithfulness, gentleness, and self-control . . . these aren't traits we manufacture—they're the result of abiding. When we stay connected to the Vine, His life flows through ours and fruit begins to form.

We often assume that in order to testify, we have to be loud or eloquent or have it all together. But sometimes the most powerful testimony is a quiet life that has been shaped by consistent presence. The fruit of faithfulness. The evidence of someone who's stayed.

Sometimes the most powerful testimony is a quiet life that has been shaped by consistent presence.

Jesus ends this verse by pointing out to the disciples that their relationship with Him is what qualifies them to testify: "because you have been with me from the beginning."

The same is true for you. You don't need a theology degree or years of church leadership experience to talk about Jesus. Your relationship with Him—your journey, your story—is enough. You've been chosen, called, and equipped by Him.

Sometimes, we hold back because we think we need to be "ready" or "better equipped." But the truth is, we'll never feel 100 percent ready. That's why we have the Holy Spirit. When we remain in Him, we're equipped to testify—not because of who we are but because of who He is.

Sharing your testimony is an act of love. It's a way to reflect Jesus's love to the world and to invite others into the hope and joy you've found in Him. So don't wait for the perfect moment or the "right" circumstances. Start where you are. Even as a work in progress, you can point to Jesus. The beauty is often found in the becoming. And remember, testifying isn't about you. It's about Him. It's about pointing people to the One who saves, heals, and restores. So, lean on the Holy Spirit, speak with boldness, and trust that He will work through you.

If today finds you in a season of remaining—where things feel unseen, slow, or quiet—don't underestimate what God is doing in you. The fruit may not be obvious yet, but it's forming. The story may not feel finished, but it's unfolding. And one day, maybe even without trying, your life will speak clearly of the One who was with you through it all.

That's the power of remaining. That's the promise of having been with Him from the beginning.

Reflection Questions

1. What changes have you seen in yourself as a result of remaining close to Jesus?

2. Think about someone whose life testifies to their closeness with Jesus. What stands out to you about the fruit they bear?

3. What does it mean to you to be "with Jesus," not just in belief but in practice?

Conclusion

Keep On Keeping On

This is it—our final day together in this devotional. And I just want to say thank you. Thank you for showing up, for leaning into this rhythm, for letting God work in your heart through these past thirty days. It's been an honor to walk this journey with you, to pray with you, and to reflect on His truth together.

But just because you've reached the last day doesn't mean the journey is over. Release, rest, and remain aren't just themes for these devotionals—they are a rhythm for life. One that you'll keep returning to, over and over again. You won't always get it right. There will be days when you hold on too tightly, when rest feels impossible, when remaining in Him feels like work instead of worship.

And yet, His invitation stands.

When your heart feels heavy—release.

When the noise of life overwhelms you—rest.

When doubt creeps in—remain.

Not perfectly but faithfully.

Because this rhythm of release, rest, and remain has never been about getting it all right. It's about drawing near to the One who already has. It's about proximity, not perfection. And the beauty of remaining is that the closer you stay to Him, the more you begin to reflect Him. His love shapes you. His truth anchors you. His Spirit strengthens you.

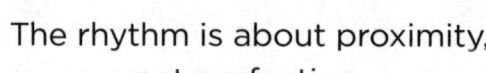

The rhythm is about proximity, not perfection.

So, as you step forward from these thirty days, my prayer for you is this:

That you would continue to release what was never yours to carry.

That you would find deep, soul-refreshing rest in His presence.

That you would remain—through every high and every low—knowing that He remains with you, always.

And because I know these rhythms are easier said than done, I want to leave you with something practical—a way to return to these truths whenever you need to realign your heart. As you walk through the guide, may you always remember that you are never alone, that grace is always available, and that His joy and strength are yours, today and always.

The Rhythm of Release, Rest, and Remain

Whether you're walking through joy or struggle, celebration or sorrow, imagine yourself back on that walk with Jesus, listening to Him speak to you. Picture yourself in His presence, carrying those burdens, hopes, and questions. As you reflect on His words, walk through the rhythm of release, rest, and remain.

Release

READ: John 15:1–8 (either in your Bible or on page 8)

PRAY: God, You see what I'm holding and how tightly I've been gripping it. I want to trust You with it, even though it feels uncertain. I release it into Your hands, not because it's easy, but because I know You are good. You are the Gardener who prunes with purpose. Shape me. Grow me. Even when I don't understand, help me believe that what You're doing is for my good and Your glory. I let go and I lean in. In Jesus's name, amen.

WRITE: Think about your life right now. What's one burden you're carrying? What's one area of your life where you feel stuck, uncertain, or weighed down? Ask the Holy Spirit to bring that specific thing to mind. Then, in trust, write it down as an act of release—naming what you're placing into God's hands today.

_____

_____

_____

_____

_____

_____

Rest

READ: John 15:9–17 (either in your Bible or on page 66)

PRAY: God, may I rest in the truth that You are the one who brings fruit out of my life. May I rest in the reality that Your love is already mine, not something I need to hustle for or earn. May I rest in the fact that Your joy—Your complete, unshakable joy— can be mine too. Lord, I don't have to strive. I don't have to control or produce—I just have to trust. Help me trust that You're working even when I can't see it. Your command is to love, and I trust that You will love others through me. Show me how I can follow Your command to love today. In Jesus's name, amen.

WRITE: Where in your life have you been striving instead of resting in God's love? What would it look like to lay down that striving and let His love carry you instead? Write down one tangible way you will practice resting in His love—whether it's through a spiritual habit, a boundary you set, or a moment of stillness you make space for.

Remain

READ: John 15:18–27 (either in your Bible or on page 126)

PRAY: Father, I know that remaining in You is the only way to complete joy, but sometimes it's just plain hard. The world is loud. It's distracting. It pulls me in every direction, making promises it can't keep. But I don't want to chase after things that won't last. I want to stay with You.

Help me choose You—again and again—especially when it's hard. When I get tired, remind me that You are my strength. When I get distracted, pull my focus back to You. And when I start to waver, let Your Spirit anchor me in truth.

Holy Spirit, be my guide. Remind me of Jesus's words, fill me with wisdom, and give me the courage to testify about who You are—not just with my words but with my life. Thank You for never leaving me to figure this out on my own. I'm holding on to You. I'm remaining in You.

In Jesus's name, amen.

WRITE: Write down one area of your life where you're struggling to remain in Him. How can you choose to place Him above that area? What's one way you can testify about His love this week?

_____

_____

_____

_____

_____

_____

_____

Acknowledgments

To God: Thank You for staying close, even when I felt distant. For being present in the silence. For whispering truth when I couldn't hear it and holding me when I didn't know I needed to be held. During our time on Fox Island, You not only cared for me but You cared for little Yvette, too, just as You always have. You didn't rush the healing. You met us both with gentleness. Thank You for being the God who sees, stays, and heals in ways I didn't know I needed.

To little Yvette: Thank you for hanging in there. For holding on while I tried to manage everything. You worked so hard to stay small, to be good, to not ask for too much. But you didn't have to prove your worth—you were already chosen, already loved. In the quiet, God met us—tending gently, pruning what couldn't stay, making room for something new to grow. You didn't need to be hidden. You needed to be held. And He's been holding us both the whole time. I see you now. I'm learning to walk with you—rooted, not restless, remaining in the One who never let go.

To my husband, Glen Henry: Thank you for your extraordinary love and sacrifice. In a season of deep grief, when you needed me most, you gave me the space to tend to my own soul. It was in that gift of release that I discovered this rhythm—release, rest, and remain—and this devotional would not be what it is without that discovery. In letting me go, you allowed me to encounter God's presence in a profound way, reminding me that He was always there, even when I thought I had to strive to find Him.

To my children, Theophilus, Uriah, Anaya, and Uziah: Thank you for your patience as I stepped away to write, for the times you asked about this devotional, for the curiosity and love you showed me even amid deadlines. I had to say no to things I wish I could have said yes to, and yet you met me with so much understanding. My deepest hope is that one day the rhythm of release, rest, and remain will become part of your own walk with the Lord.

To my parents, John and Ann Givens: Thank you for laying the foundation of my faith and introducing me to the Lord. That gift is one I will always carry with me.

To my big brother, Anthony O'Neal: Thank you for seeing something in me before I fully saw it in myself. Your belief that I had something worthwhile to say and your willingness to connect me to my agent played such a key role in this journey.

To my agent, Alex Field: Thank you for coming alongside me and guiding me through this process with such care. From shaping the book proposal to championing this message, you believed in this rhythm and in my words; that has meant so much to me.

To my editor, Kim Von Fange: This devotional would not be what it is without your insight, encouragement, and patience. You challenged me to go deeper, and in doing so, you pulled out something I didn't even know was there. I am so grateful for you.

To every person who played a role in bringing this devotional to life—from early conversations to refining ideas, shaping the manuscript, editing the words, and designing the pages: Thank you. Whether your name appears here or not, your contribution is felt and deeply appreciated. You helped carry this message, and I'm so grateful.

To my family, friends, and online community: Thank you for cheering me on through the quiet and the chaos. For your prayers, your texts, your encouragement, and your presence. You reminded me that I wasn't alone, and that reminder often came exactly when I needed it most.

And to you, the reader: Thank you for trusting me with a small part of your journey. I pray these words met you with grace and truth. That you felt seen. That you felt less alone. And that, no matter what season you're in, the rhythm of release, rest, and remain becomes not just something you've read but something you live—with gentleness, with hope, and with God ever near.

ABOUT THE AUTHOR

YVETTE HENRY is a wife, homeschooling mother of four, speaker, writer, and content creator based in Southern California. She co-hosts the *How Married Are You?!* podcast with her husband and shares her family's journey on their YouTube channel, Beleaf In Fatherhood. Through storytelling and encouragement, Yvette creates spaces for women to embrace authentic womanhood and remain rooted in Christ.

Her devotional, *Release, Rest, Remain,* was birthed from a season of deep exhaustion and a longing for lasting peace. Through the simple yet powerful rhythm of releasing, resting, and remaining, she invites readers to draw near to the Lord and trust Him to do the rest.

When she's not writing or creating, Yvette enjoys chasing sunsets, soaking in the beauty of nature, or resting in her hammock.